SOAKING
— *IN THE* —
SPIRIT

DESTINY IMAGE BOOKS BY CAROL ARNOTT

Preparing for the Glory

SOAKING
— *IN THE* —
SPIRIT

*Effortless Access to Hearing
God's Voice, Intimacy with the Father,
and Supernatural Healing*

CAROL ARNOTT

DESTINY IMAGE® PUBLISHERS, INC.

P.O. Box 310, Shippensburg, PA 17257-0310

"Promoting Inspired Lives."

This book and all other Destiny Image and Destiny Image Fiction books are available at Christian bookstores and distributors worldwide.

Cover design by Eileen Rockwell
Interior design by Terry Clifton

For more information on foreign distributors, call 717-532-3040.

Reach us on the Internet: www.destinyimage.com.

ISBN 13 TP: 978-0-7684-4880-1
ISBN 13 eBook: 978-0-7684-4881-8
ISBN 13 HC: 978-0-7684-4883-2
ISBN 13 LP: 978-0-7684-4882-5

For Worldwide Distribution, Printed in the U.S.A.

1 2 3 4 5 6 7 8 / 24 23 22 21 20

CONTENTS

FOREWORD

by Beni Johnson

In 1996, I had a life-changing encounter with God. Revival had hit John and Carol Arnott's church, Toronto Airport Christian Fellowship, and Bill and I traveled there with my parents. While we weren't feeling particularly burned out, we were hungry to know more of God. We carried a holy dissatisfaction, passionate to see everything God had for us manifested in our lives. After one evening session, I was hit with the power of God in a way that I had never experienced before. I shook on the floor for 20 minutes, unable to stand. The Lord shook the strongholds right out of my life and, as He later explained to me, birthed my true identity. I was completely changed. Bill likes to say that he went to Toronto with a lamb, but he came home with a lioness!

Spending time in the presence of God does just that for each of us. After my encounter, fear had no place of authority in my life. In the presence of Light, darkness cannot remain.

When I returned from our trip to Toronto, I began to practice soaking for the first time. With my focus set on adoring God, I would allow all of my attention to be in communion with Him. I was totally in love; I simply wanted to be with Him. I began to learn how to connect with the Holy Spirit and dwell in the presence of God without an agenda. A deep well of intimacy began to develop in my spirit and, to this day, this practice is a pivotal part of my walk with the Lord.

Carol's new book, *Soaking in the Spirit*, is a powerful teaching on the practice of soaking in God's presence. Interweaving her own testimony with strong biblical teaching and practical wisdom, this book is an invitation to grow in relationship with God. Carol explains how, by setting aside time to saturate in His presence, we actually become more like Jesus, better equipped to pour out onto a world that is dying to know the Father.

It is the absolute grace of God that, as we draw closer to Jesus, He reorients us back to Himself and His original design for our lives. This is what soaking is about: an intimate relationship with God, through which we cannot remained unchanged.

John and Carol's obedience in following the direction of the Holy Spirit transformed my spiritual life. I would encourage every believer to read *Soaking in the Spirit*. It carries a vital message for our current culture. Let the testimonies in this book stir your spirit and encourage you to protect space in the busyness of life to rest in the presence of God. Let His presence fill you so that the Body of Christ can truly release the kingdom and bring heaven to earth.

BENI JOHNSON
Bethel Church, Redding, CA
Author of *The Power of Communion*, *Healthy & Free*,
and *The Happy Intercessor*

FOREWORD

by Heidi Baker

Soaking in the Spirit: Effortless Access to Hearing God's Voice, Intimacy with the Father, and Supernatural Healing by Carol Arnott is a book about being in God's presence in an intentional and life-changing way. Soaking is a concept that can be hard to wrap your head around, but this beautiful book brings it to a practical and personal level. You will want to jump right in to God's glorious presence even as you read. Soaking prayer is not a strange thing just for extreme Christians; it is for everyone.

God already knows every thought, prayer, and concern that passes through your mind, but relationships are built through communication. We are called to be intentional in communication with Holy Spirit to know Him and understand His ways—that takes time. In the presence, we are transformed, our hearts are healed, our minds renewed, and our spirits lifted. Throughout the book, you will read personal stories of the impact of soaking on Carol and others, for heart transformation and also for physical healing. You will also get practical advice on how to soak and make soaking a lifestyle.

Paul calls all of us to pray without ceasing. This feels impossible until you learn that we can pray our way through whatever we are doing. In Mozambique, where I live, we want to do everything from the presence. We spend a great deal of time in prayer, soaking, worshipping and interceding because we want Heaven's strategies, not just our own strength. What does that look like practically?

On Tuesdays we have staff meetings in the morning around 10:00am. I wake up around 5am and start my day with a prayer walk seeking God's word for the day. Then I go to a prayer room on our base next to our home and meet with friends on our team to pray and worship together, often soaking in His presence then praying. Next, we all head over to staff meeting and worship together. We pray as a group, in our departments or in small groups as God leads. We pray for those who are heading out on outreaches, sometimes into dangerous areas. We pray for anyone who is sick or struggling. Honestly, by the time we get to agenda points, God has already met us in a deep way and there is not too much left to plan!

I lead discipleship for our children once a week, and I disciple some of our pastors and leaders. In both groups, we start with worship and prayer, then go through Bible teaching and practical application in our lives, and end by praying for one another. In outreach meetings, we pray over the map of Mozambique as we decide where to share the Gospel each week. For the university, many of our visitors want to take a tour of the campus. We start at the prayer room with every group. Together with our Mozambican team, we pray and prophesy over the university, then we finish the tour. We all get so encouraged every time as Holy Spirit gives more vision and confirmation. In these ways, we really do pray without ceasing as we cover each of our programs in prayer.

You can do the same thing in your life, spending intentional quiet times in prayer soaking and also praying throughout your day. Especially pray over decisions you need to make, groups you work with, and tasks you need to complete. God wants to be part of every area of your life, and it's so much easier to work when you get wisdom from Holy Spirit.

In Iris Global, we work very hard. We are passionate about feeding the hungry, digging wells, building churches and schools, starting a university, and many other things, but all of those ideas were birthed and carried out in prayer. We love God deeply and our lives are a love offering to Him. God wants a relationship with you, beloved. Carol spends a section of this book talking about how we are not servants, we are lovers. When she and John were dating, all she wanted to do was talk to him for hours. Making him a cup of tea was a joy, not a chore. God doesn't want us to slave away to change this world. He wants to fill us to overflowing with His love, His joy and His presence. When we are full, everything we do is saturated with love. The people we minister to can truly tell the difference. They don't want dry, grouchy people telling them about God's love. What impact would that have? We get filled up in His presence, and then we love this world with His all-powerful, transformative love.

For Carol, soaking other people in prayer is a powerful part of her personal ministry. She testifies about powerful miracles that happened just from spending the time to soak with people, especially those in need of emotional and/or physical healing. Soaking also makes us more familiar with what Holy Spirit is saying to help us know how to pray for other people and see them set free. Today, soaking prayer, prophecy, speaking in tongues, laughter, falling down, and other manifestations of Holy Spirit are more common, but back in the 1990s, this was all new territory. As John and Carol stewarded this move of God, a group of us became very close friends. We intentionally joined together to support one another and speak into each other's lives. Those relationships are very dear to me.

All of us loved God and gave our lives away for love before this revival started, but we didn't know Holy Spirit in this intimate way. My husband, Rolland, and I were missionaries in Asia, UK, and Mozambique before the Toronto Blessing ever occurred. We were fully devoted to God, preaching, praying, leading people to Jesus and meeting the practical needs of the poor as Jesus taught us to do. John and Carol were pastors faithfully teaching, serving and loving God's people. They cared deeply for God, their congregation and their city. None of us expected all that would take place in Toronto. It was beyond anything we could imagine, and it took us by surprise. Holy God sovereignly poured out His Spirit in a tangible way on His people, and we all learned and grew together through this season. Many people around the world were forever changed by radical God encounters in Toronto.

Rolland and I both had experiences there that completely transformed our lives and our ministry. Our hearts were the first things that had to change—that was what allowed our ministry to change. You have to let God transform you first from the inside out, then He can use you in powerful ways. One of the core messages of my life is "all fruitfulness flows from intimacy," a statement grounded in John 15. We can't love others well when we don't feel loved. We can't feel love unless we abide in Him. For me, God stuck me to the ground for seven days and nights and also radically healed me from near-death sickness. He showed me powerful visions and spoke to my heart. Rolland changed from a grouchy man to "Tigger," laughing and jumping for joy. Then our ministry grew from several churches to thousands of churches, from hard work and striving to joy and presence. It was not suddenly easy, but when you're in love, you can do anything. Ministering from God's overflow and presence is vastly different than working day and night feeling exhausted and dry. I'm forever grateful for those encounters. They led us into a lifestyle of soaking and being in God's presence in the midst of everything we need to get done. We are much more productive now.

In the midst of this, Carol and I got very close. I love her deeply, and we pray for one another on a regular basis. She and John called me with a strong prophetic word that might have saved my life a couple of years ago. Covenant friends who can speak into our lives with what they hear God saying are critical as we step out in radical ways for God. There is strength in unity and confirmations. We are not called to live this life of faith on our own. We need each other. We are grateful for John and Carol. We love to minister together and spend hours soaking in the presence together. I learn immensely from their laid-down lives of love.

I know you will also learn from Carol's life as she vulnerably shares her journey and experiences in this book. I encourage you to make soaking prayer a part of your daily life. If you can read the book and practice soaking with your friends or small group, even better. Use the activations to get started. I promise you, time in God's presence is never wasted. He longs for you to know how much He loves you and how deeply He cares about all the things you care about. His desire is for everything you do to flow from this Love. He is a Good, Good Father. Now dive in and start your soaking adventure with God!

HEIDI G. BAKER PH.D.
Co-founder and Executive Chairman of Iris Global

Chapter 1

GETTING TO KNOW THE PRESENCE OF GOD

WHEN I MET THE HOLY SPIRIT

When God crashed in on my life, it was completely unexpected. I was a single mother with two boys, a two-year-old and a four-year-old and life was tough. My husband had left us, he was an emotionally abusive and self-centered, unpredictable person and he continued to make things difficult for us. I felt vulnerable, afraid and alone. One evening as I stood in the bathroom brushing my teeth, I heard an audible voice speaking to me. At first, I thought it was my ex-husband breaking into my house again. I left the bathroom and quickly checked throughout the whole house, even the basement and garage, but everything was fine. I went back to my bathroom and I heard the voice again. I thought I was having a nervous breakdown, as I was now hearing voices. I threw the toothbrush in the sink and shouted, "All right, I'll listen!" As I listened, I realized that the voice was speaking audibly the 23rd Psalm to me—not in my head, but as if a person was standing in the room. Halfway through the Psalm, I realized that it was Jesus talking to me. I suddenly knew that He loved me in all my sin, in all my fears and in all my pain. In floods of tears I ran to my bedroom and found my little white confirmation Bible with a zipper around it. I opened it and found the words that Jesus had been speaking to me:

The Lord is my shepherd;

I shall not want.

He makes me to lie down in green pastures;

He leads me beside the still waters.

He restores my soul;

He leads me in the paths of righteousness

For His name's sake.

As I read, Jesus flooded me with waves of incredible love and joy. I didn't know that I needed to be "born again," but that night I said yes to Jesus and gave my life to Him. From then on, it was a wonderful adventure getting to know Him. My circumstances didn't change, but somehow the grass was greener, the sky was bluer and a deep fountain of incredible joy was bubbling up inside of me. I would kneel down at my bed and pray and this beautiful presence would come and as I prayed, it would increase. I grew up in the Lutheran church and I remembered the pastor talking about God the Father, God the Son, but only about God the Holy Ghost in hushed tones. As a little girl, I knew what a ghost was, but not a holy one! There was never any teaching about who the Holy Ghost was or that we could experience Him. So when I became a Christian, I had no paradigm for getting to know the Holy Spirit. I thought that the presence I was experiencing during prayer was the presence of Jesus.

It wasn't until I went to a Kathryn Kuhlman meeting that I found out about the Holy Spirit. Kathryn was an amazing evangelist and healing minister and she would talk about the Holy Spirit as this wonderful person of the Trinity who wanted to be with us. She would say, "He's more real to me than any human being."[1] I didn't fully understand what she was saying, but I knew that I wanted so much to know about this third person of the Trinity, so began my quest. I read books about the Holy Spirit and they taught about being filled with the Holy Spirit. Their instructions were to open my mouth to receive and I would be filled with the Holy Spirit. So night after night I would kneel down on my bed and open my mouth, but nothing seemed to happen. I kept praying and searching for more because I really wanted to know the Holy Spirit in the way Kathryn Kuhlman had described.

I went up for every altar call to be baptized in the Holy Spirit. Nothing seemed to happen until a friend told me that there was a man named John Arnott who was going to be preaching in a little white church near Stratford and invited me to come with her. I came, and at the end of the sermon, John said, "There's someone here who has been absolutely seeking, desiring, and praying for the baptism of the Holy Spirit." I was like the roadrunner that night! I ran straight to the front of the church. John prayed for me and I got absolutely immersed in the presence of the Holy Spirit. I was filled from the top of my head, down to my toes. I began speaking in tongues and I couldn't stop. Even if I tried, I couldn't speak English. At the end of the meeting, I went home and spoke in tongues until I couldn't stay awake any longer. I woke up a few hours later and opened my mouth and I still couldn't speak English. I spoke in tongues for another couple of hours and went back to sleep for another hour. It was an incredible experience. I was filled with the love, joy, and peace of God's presence and I didn't want it to stop there. After that, I continued to pursue getting to know the Holy Spirit. It has been such a delightful journey.

WHO IS HE?

I want to introduce you to that wonderful third person of the Trinity, the Holy Spirit. Like me, you may be aware of God the Father, and Jesus, the loving Son and Bridegroom, but less acquainted with the Holy Spirit.

The Holy Spirit is a person. He is gentle, forgiving, and long-suffering. He is called the Comforter and He truly is the most wonderful friend and companion. In John 16, we see that the Holy Spirit brings the words of Jesus to our remembrance and convicts the world of sin. He guides us into all truth; He is the Spirit of truth and the giver of life. He is our teacher. He will help you understand the Bible and lead you in your prayer life. He wants to communicate with you. Just ask Him, "Holy Spirit, teach me how to pray." He always knows what to say.

The Holy Spirit was there at creation, hovering over the waters. He was present all throughout the Bible and He is still with us. He is around us, He can fill us, and He can come on us in power. In John 16, Jesus told His disciples that if He didn't go to the Father, the Holy Spirit wouldn't come. Jesus told us that the Holy Spirit will never leave us or forsake us (see John 14:16). I know that to be so true. Whether I've been sick, tired, or jet-lagged, whether I've been feeling horrible or feeling really good, the Holy Spirit has never ever, let me down. He has always been a faithful friend and companion.

The Holy Spirit helps us to love Jesus and to know the Father. He is the most wonderful person, yet He is holy and also very powerful! His power raised Jesus from the dead and He empowers us to live an abundant, joyful, powerful Christian life.

If we want to please the heart of God, it's so important to recognize that the Holy Spirit has feelings. When we are critical and judgmental of others, when we're proud, when we're bitter, and when our words aren't pleasing to the Father, it grieves Him (see Eph. 4:30). Ask the Holy Spirit to watch your thoughts and your heart, because it's so easy to be critical and judgmental. If we give Him permission to speak into our lives and ask Him if we've hurt Him, He will always answer that prayer. We must remember the law of sowing and reaping. In Matthew 6, Jesus tells us that if we

> If we want to please the heart of God, it's so important to recognize that the Holy Spirit has feelings.

judge other people, we'll also be judged by God. So we want to stay out of that place of criticism and judgment of others.

It hurts the Holy Spirit when we don't love each other like He loves us. We're called to forgive everybody. Of course, forgiveness is not the same as trust. We can forgive and ask for love for a person who has hurt us, but that doesn't mean that you have to trust a person who has hurt you deeply.

It pleases the Holy Spirit when we love Jesus and when we bear good fruit. He actually enables us to become like Jesus—full of love, joy, peace, patience, kindness, goodness, faithfulness, gentleness, and self-control (see Gal. 5:22-23). His presence in your life will cause you to be more thankful, more loving, and more unified with others.

THE HOLY SPIRIT WANTS RELATIONSHIP

When I was getting to know the Holy Spirit, I discovered that as I worshipped Jesus, the Holy Spirit would draw close. The Holy Spirit loves to glorify Jesus and He loves it when we love Jesus too. In John 16:14 we read that Jesus glorifies the Father and the Holy Spirit glorifies Jesus. Have you ever experienced more of the Holy Spirit as you worship? That's because He wants you to worship Jesus. The more we love Jesus, the more the Holy Spirit will come.

The Holy Spirit wants to be near to us. He wants to have a relationship with us that runs deep. Jesus said, *"The world cannot accept Him, because it neither sees Him nor knows Him. But you know Him, for He lives with you and will be in you"* (John 14:17 NIV). It's not a five-minute fling. When a couple is dating or engaged, they only have eyes for the other person. They spend time with each other, getting to know each other. They want to develop a deep relationship. That's what the Holy Spirit wants to do with you. He is with you and in you and He wants you to get to know Him intimately. Building that relationship is going to take time, in the good days and the bad days. He'll ask you to do things, and as you choose obedience, you'll build with Him and learn to trust Him more. It's such a wonderful adventure. Once you begin to know and love this beautiful person and depend on Him for your strength, your prayer life, and for reading the Bible, you will become a changed person. People will see Jesus in you.

Have you ever experienced that you feel more of the Holy Spirit as you worship? That's because He wants you to worship Jesus. The more we love Jesus, the more the Holy Spirit will come.

R.T. Kendall talks about the Holy Spirit as a dove who is easily hurt and sensitive.[2] Picture the Holy Spirit like a dove sitting on your shoulder. Bill Johnson talks about the Holy Spirit as a dove that rests on your shoulder.[3] How would you behave if you had a real dove sitting on your shoulder and you didn't want it to fly away? You'd be very aware of all of your movements and very careful about what you said. In these end times, the Holy Spirit wants to come in power and He wants people He can trust, who are sensitive and aware of His presence. I want to be a child of God on whom the Holy Spirit will rest. I want Him to fill me and absolutely permeate my life. Do you?

EXPERIENCE IS A GOOD THING

Throughout the years, I've heard people tell me, "You think it's all about experience." What those people often mean is that we shouldn't go after experiences with the Holy Spirit. They're saying that it's a bad thing to want an experiential relationship with God. Often these people are afraid that if others are encouraged to experience God, they will disregard God's Word and biblical ways of living. My husband, John, and I have never said that it's only about experiences with God. We need both the Word and the Spirit in equal measure. Many believers also think that the Holy Spirit stopped moving and working at the end of the Acts of the Apostles. That couldn't be further from the truth!

The Bible is a book of history, prophecy, law, poetry, and teaching. All of it comes out of the experiences of its lead characters. In the same way, your life needs to be comprised of experiences with the Holy Spirit along with being guided in the Word. That only happens by spending time together. The Bible says that *"God is love"* (1 John 4:8). Love is an intimate, experiential thing. Jesus also said, *"You shall love the*

Lord your God with all your heart, with all your soul, with all your strength, and with all your mind" (Luke 10:27). The first way we must love God is with our hearts. Loving Him with all of our heart, soul, strength, and mind doesn't sound like a passive action. Loving God with everything in us will definitely be full of emotions and experiences.

In Mark 1:8, John the Baptist said, *"I indeed baptized you with water, but He will baptize you with the Holy Spirit."* We can get to know the Holy Spirit by being baptized in Him and filled with His presence. When you ask for more of the Holy Spirit, He hears you and answers you.

My good friend Heidi Baker came to our church in 1997 as a burnt-out missionary. She was a systematic theologian who took herself very seriously. Heidi had grown up with terrible dyslexia. As a child, she couldn't read the words on a page and she was ridiculed for her disability. It was a painful and humiliating experience. At 13 years old, she was

The Bible is a book of history, prophecy, law, poetry, and teaching. All of it comes out of the experiences of its lead characters.

miraculously healed, and as an adult she worked incredibly hard to earn multiple degrees. When she walked into our church to find out what the Holy Spirit was doing, she absolutely did not want to fall on the floor or be embarrassed. But the Lord had other plans. The Holy Spirit hit her dramatically, and for a solid week, she was on the floor, pasted down.

She was like a jellyfish. She couldn't stand. God moved in her life radically that week. He began to heal her heart from all the burnout that she had experienced and gave her a vision for the country of Mozambique. That experience started a love affair with the Holy Spirit. Now Heidi and her husband, Rolland, are the leaders of Iris Ministries, with schools, outreaches, homes for orphans, and thousands of churches around the world. She could not have done all that without a dramatic experience of God renewing her heart and life, followed by a lifestyle built around relationship with Him.

Being filled with the Holy Spirit did an incredible thing for this woman of God! He wants that kind of relationship with you. Are you willing? He is looking for individuals who will spend time with Him. When Heidi came to our church she didn't want to be mocked or embarrassed, and you can understand from her childhood why. But God healed her and asked, "Will you let me do what I want?" and she said "Yes," not knowing what would happen.

Melinda Fish says, "There are no toxic levels of the Holy Spirit." The more time we spend in His presence, experiencing Him, the more we will be filled with Him and it will never be a waste of time. You can't give away what you haven't already received from Him.

COMMON MISUNDERSTANDINGS

I've prayed for so many people to be filled with the Holy Spirit that I can't even count them all! Over the years, I've seen some common misunderstandings that people have about experiencing God's presence.

I Can't Feel Him

When I pray for somebody in a meeting, they often look for a strong physical manifestation. They're looking at what's going on in the room around them and thinking, "Well, I'm not feeling anything, so nothing is happening." God can be moving in you whether or not you feel anything, but oftentimes, they're not actually in tune with the small ways that God is moving in their body.

If this is something you've experienced, it's important to learn to quiet yourself down and tune into what the Holy Spirit is doing. We can be so in tune with our minds that we don't feel what's going on in our bodies. We need to learn to tune into the Holy Spirit's wonderful peace. I'll often ask people, "Are you feeling peace on you?" and they'll say, "Well, yeah, I am." I always encourage them to welcome that, because what they're feeling is the Holy Spirit. They might think a feeling of peace is insignificant, but it's not at all. Jesus is the Prince of Peace and experiencing His peace is a wonderful manifestation of His presence.

John never used to feel anything when the Holy Spirit moved, but I taught him to tune in to the ways that the Holy Spirit comes. I'd pray for him regularly, two or three times a day, and encourage him to quiet his mind and tune into the Holy Spirit. As I prayed for him, I'd feel the flow of the Holy

Spirit going into him, but then something strange would happen. It felt almost like a kink in a hose when the water comes back up the hose. I'd say, "Where did you go?" and he'd ask, "What do you mean?" I'd say, "Well, your mind went somewhere because I could feel the Holy Spirit come back on me." He had gotten distracted and was thinking about something other than focusing on Jesus and receiving.

So John began to trust that I could really feel the Holy Spirit going into him. That helped him relax more and he would drink in His presence. Now he feels the Holy Spirit's presence on his hands, especially in worship. He's more tuned into his body and his feelings.

Jesus is The Prince of Peace and experiencing His peace is a wonderful manifestation of His presence.

When I'm praying for people, I'll also ask them if they feel a weight or tingling in their hands. Sometimes they might feel a weight on their head. It can be so slight, that if you're not looking out for it, you can miss it. But whenever you feel that, ask the Holy Spirit for more and it will increase. Honour every little way that you experience the Holy Spirit and He will be delighted to show you more of Himself..

I Feel Afraid

Many people have a fear of receiving from the Holy Spirit, especially if they've been abused. Opening yourself up to the Holy Spirit is a vulnerable thing to do and that can be scary. If I'm praying for someone, I can tell if they're afraid of falling down under the power of the Holy Spirit. Of course, I'm not going to force anyone to fall down or lie down, but I've found that standing for a long time to receive can be tiring, so I'll often encourage these people to sit if they don't want to lie down. The important thing is to quiet yourself down, stop the busyness and bring your mind into just loving Him and receiving from Him.

I Want to Stay in Control

Maybe because of fear, or other negative life experiences, many people want to stay in control rather than letting the Holy Spirit move as He wants to. When I'm praying for them, they might speak in tongues continuously, trying to make something happen, so I'll ask them not to pray in tongues but to stay quiet, to take a couple of deep breaths of the Holy Spirit who is all around them and receive. I encourage them that they can pray in the Spirit later. Tongues is an amazing way to pour out to God, but not when learning to receive and take His presence in. The same would apply for praying in your native language.

When I can tell that someone wants to stay in control rather than yield to God's presence, I'll ask them, "You've invited the Holy Spirit into your heart, haven't you? You've given Him control, so you just need to step back. You might think the Holy Spirit is going to knock you off your feet, but it's about yielding. Take deep breaths. His presence is here."

They'll say, "He is?" I'll ask them if they're feeling His

Jesus tells us to abide in Him. That's not a suggestion; that's a command.

peace and they'll say, "Yes, I am actually!" I'll encourage them to breathe in the peace of His presence and let it go deep. Sometimes, after two or three breaths they might fear that they'll fall and they decide to take control back. So I always tell them to continue to yield. The Holy Spirit is a safe person. And if you don't feel anything, that's okay. Just

say, "Holy Spirit, I've come to love Jesus, please help me to love Him."

WE'RE CALLED TO ABIDE

I love this passage, John 15:1-8:

> *I am the true vine, and my Father is the gardener. He cuts off every branch in me that bears no fruit, while every branch that does bear fruit he prunes so that it will be even more fruitful. You are already clean because of the word I have spoken to you. Remain in me, as I also remain in you. No branch can bear fruit by itself; it must remain in the vine. Neither can you bear fruit unless you remain in me.*

I am the vine; you are the branches. If you remain in me and I in you, you will bear much fruit; apart from me you can do nothing. If you do not remain in me, you are like a branch that is thrown away and withers; such branches are picked up, thrown into the fire and burned. If you remain in me and my words remain in you, ask whatever you wish, and it will be done for you. This is to my Father's glory, that you bear much fruit, showing yourselves to be my disciples (John 15:1-8 NIV).

Jesus tells us to abide in Him. That's not a suggestion; that's a command. We all want to lead fruitful Christian lives, but first, we must spend time with Jesus. Many believers skip right to the end of this passage, *"This is to my Father's glory, that you bear much fruit."* But they forget the first part. Abiding comes first. That's where we become anointed and filled to do what Jesus is calling us to do.

Abiding means staying, waiting, and remaining. It's a continuous thing. It's not instant. I've learned in my life that abiding in God's presence will totally transform your relationship with your Saviour, your Bridegroom, and your King, and it will empower you to bring the kingdom with mighty signs and wonders.

Imagine! God Almighty, the God of the universe wants to love you. When you look at the beauty of God's creation and the incredible detail in the Bible, you realize how intelligent and amazingly powerful God is. That same God wants to spend time with us, He wants to love us and to abide with us. Isn't He wonderful!

ACTIVATION

I really believe in the power of prayer ministry. Over the years, John and I have seen that people who take time to receive prayer after a sermon in a church service receive a lot more than just hearing the message and going on with their day. I think the same applies to reading books. You have an opportunity to let the message go from your head to your heart. That's why, at the end of each chapter, I'll include an activation. It will include some questions to ask yourself, some questions to ask God in prayer and journaling, and some practical applications and prayers. Instead of just reading a chapter and going on with your day, take time to let God speak to you and transform you.

Do you feel like you relate to God more as Father, Son, or Holy Spirit? Take some time to ponder and ask God whether you've been unaware of the wonderful third person of the Trinity.

Invite Him to move in your life again. Do you want to be filled with the Holy Spirit? To have a deep relationship with Him? To abide with Him? Simply ask God: "Father, I want to be immersed in that wonderful presence. Help me to know the wonderful person of the Holy Spirit." Take time to wait on Him and abide with Him today.

Where has control or fear hindered you from experiencing the Holy Spirit? Repent for those decisions today. Tell Him, "God, I want to feel and to experience you. Teach me, nurture me in feeling and experiencing your presence. I welcome you to move in my life."

NOTES

1. Roberts Liardon, R. (2005). *Kathryn Kuhlman: A Spiritual Biography of God's Miracle Worker.* (New Kensington, Pennsylvania, PA: Whitaker House, 2005).

2. R.T. Kendall, *The Sensitivity of the Holy Spirit* (Lake Mary, FL: Charisma House, 2002).

3. Bill Johnson, B. (2012). *Manifesto for a Normal Christian Life.* [Kindle Ed.]. (Bethel, CA: Bill Johnson Ministries).

Chapter 2

SOAKING IS ABOUT RELATIONSHIP

Making Time to Abide

We all get so busy doing. Life seems to throw a million things at us at once. It's so easy to become tired and burnt out and weary in well doing. Soaking is the antidote to that. It is an opportunity to abide in the presence of God. When I soak, I position myself before God to abide in Him. Soaking is purposefully making space to be together with the Lord and to receive from Him. No matter how busy your life is, no matter what else you have going on, it's never a waste of time.

The Circle of Our Lives

Jesus told us that the first commandment is to love the Lord with all your heart and to love others as you love yourself (see Matt. 22:37-39). There are three areas of love—love the Lord, love yourself and love other people. It is much like a circle, At first we just come before Him and let Jesus pour out His love for us, then we get filled and learn to love ourselves as He loves us. From there we are able to pour out our love back to Him. But then we realize the lost are really lost and begin to turn our attention to loving and gathering the lost. His love that has transformed our hearts, burdens us to see that same freedom come to those around us. This emphasis is constantly moving one to the other, not dwelling in one place. Like the circle with a rotating emphasis on Me-Him-Them.

We need to be filled up with God's love and presence so that we can love Him and love others. That's our whole purpose. If you're not filled up, then you can't give anything away, and if you don't give anything away, that's not healthy either. You become like stagnant water. There must be a constant flow of love in our lives.

The first thing that we're called to is to love God, but we can't do that well if we're weary or burnt out. So we need to make time to love Him and to connect with Him. Ideally, we need all three things happening at once—pouring out our love on God, receiving love for ourselves, and giving love to others. I think it's a balance that we'll always be trying to figure out. In some seasons, you'll be more focused on loving God. Sometimes you'll have a season when God is healing you and you're focused on learning to love yourself, and some seasons will be all about giving love away.

Soaking helps keep us in balance with loving God, others, and ourselves. I'm going to break down these three areas. They're all very connected, so you'll see that there is a lot of overlap.

TIME FOR HIM

Soaking is positioning yourself before God, just to be together with Him intimately. God is love and He wants us to be lovers of Him and others. Intercession and prayer are so important and valuable, but there must always be time to experience His love for you and to give Him your love with no expectations or agendas. When I begin soaking, I always start with adoration. I take time to tell Him how much I love Him and to pour out my worship.

It's making time for a love affair between you and your Saviour, listening to His still small voice, and being immersed in the beautiful presence of the Holy Spirit. A love affair doesn't happen quickly; it takes time. A couple who is falling in love, spend hours chatting about nothing, getting to know each other's hearts intimately. When I have a date with John, I want to spend time with him, face to face. I know he doesn't want to hear me come with a list of things to talk about: "Well, honey, I know you want to spend time with me, but I want to talk about these other things, about my aunt, my friend, the grocery list...." That's not connecting, is it? When we spend time together, I want to know what's on his heart and how he's doing.

The first thing that we're called to is to love God, but we can't do that well if we're weary or burnt out. So we need to make time to love Him and to connect with Him.

It's the same with Jesus. When you come to soak, don't come with a shopping list of your needs. Instead, come to tell Him that you love Him, that you want to go deeper with Him. His heart's desire is to love you back and to go deep with you too. As you spend time in His presence, you'll begin to see how real He is. You'll see that He wants to have a wonderful relationship with you, that intimacy is His heart's desire. Jesus paid the highest price for you so that you might draw close to Him.

As we love on Him, we get filled up with His love and we

begin to love Jesus back. Receiving His love for us helps us love Him more. Each time you soak it will be different. Sometimes He'll flood you with His unconditional love and acceptance. Sometimes He'll heal a wound in your life. Sometimes you'll feel the heavy weighty presence of God so much that you can't move. It's all valuable and it's always worth making time for.

> Jesus paid the highest price for you so that you might draw close to Him.

If we as a church don't learn to be intimate with Him now, what is it going to be like when we get to heaven as His bride? I would think that's going to be slightly awkward! I think we're going to regret that we didn't embrace that intimacy here on earth.

RECEIVING FOR MYSELF

When we pour out our love on Him, we receive His love for us and it transforms us. The Father's love heals our wounds and our past hurts. Many of us grow up believing that God is distant, critical, and angry, but as we get to know Him, our ideas about who He is and how He loves us change. We learn that He is kind, gentle, loving, and good. Have you ever looked in the mirror and said, "I am so loved by Jesus. I am worthy. My Daddy God loves me." The first time you do it, it might be hard to look yourself in the eyes and believe it. The truth stops at your head and doesn't make its way to your heart. But as you soak, the truth of His love will sink in deep to your inner being.

Many years ago, when my dad had just died, I was laying in my reclining chair at home feeling sorry for myself. I cried out, "Oh God, I really need a dad!" and just sat there. I didn't feel like anything happened. About a week later I was at our Catch The Fire School of Ministry in Toronto, where John and I were ministering and I decided to lie down and soak after our session that morning.

Around that time, I had been reading Daniel 7:9-14, which talks about the Father, the Ancient of Days, being seated on the throne and the Son of Man, who is Jesus, being glorified in His presence. As I soaked, I had a full-on vision. In the vision, Jesus came up to me. His eyes were sparkling and twinkling. He asked me to dance. We were swirling round and round so fast that I couldn't see what was around me. As we slowed down I realized the floor was so shiny, I thought we were going to fall! I couldn't figure out where we were until I realized that we were on the Sea of Glass in heaven. In the distance, I saw the throne of God, like the throne I had read about in Daniel. It was smoking and I saw the emerald rainbow. Someone came off the throne toward us but I lost sight of Him as we danced. Then all of a sudden there was this big hand on Jesus' shoulder. It was Father God standing there. He said, "Jesus, may I dance with my daughter?" That just broke me up, I was in floods of tears. It spoke so deeply to my heart that the Father would stop what He's doing and would want to dance with His daughter. It drew my heart to Him.

Somebody could have told me that the Father really loved me, that He really cared and wanted to be with me, but a picture is worth a thousand words. I realized that my heavenly Daddy really loved me and wanted to be with me. As a child, my understanding had always been that God the Father was scary. That you had to toe the line so that you don't get punished. So as an adult, I'd taken that understanding and I'd read the Old Testament looking for the God of punishment and anger, not with the eyes of love, looking for love. That vision rewrote the truth on my heart that God is a Father who wants relationship with His people. It was a healing experience for me, especially as I was grieving the loss of my dad.

As you soak, the truth of His Love will sink in deep to your inner being.

It's so important to make time for the Lord to heal your wounds. I urge you to prioritize the healing of your heart. Make inner healing a lifestyle. King David said in Psalm 139:23-24, *"Search me, O God, and know my heart; try me,*

and know my anxieties; and see if there is any wicked way in me, and lead me in the way everlasting." This has to be a regular process for all of us. We must all let the Lord search our hearts for any unforgiveness, bitterness, pride, and pain that can so easily go unchecked. If you want to be successful in life, to cast out demons, raise the dead, to do all the wonderful things you know that Jesus has called you to and you do not deal with the issues of the heart, it will get you into difficulty. You must choose forgiveness so that the devil will not gain legal rights into your life and try to make you fall from grace and bring reproach upon Jesus. As they say, "hurting people hurt people." It's so important to break the cycle of hurt and pain by allowing the Lord to deal with your own issues.

I've spent many seasons of my life forgiving my mother and working through issues that I had as a result of our relationship. At one point, I became so frustrated and asked God, "Why don't you just set me free from my mother issues? I know you can." He revealed to me that if He did it instantly I would become prideful. Human beings tend to become full of pride and without mercy to others who are struggling with their problems. God heals us in a way that we can manage. It does take time, but it's worthwhile. He keeps us leaning on Him, sometimes walking with a limp, so that we always depend on Him for our needs.

As you soak, sometimes He will fill you with His love and you will respond with the heart of a lover. Other times He will go back and heal a deep wound. Then other times He will empower you for the ministry He has for you. Your whole life will change when you realize that the Lord absolutely loves you.

The Holy Spirit has moved so powerfully since 1994 and we have experienced the love of the Lord, His joy, and His

Your whole life will change when you realize that the Lord absolutely loves you.

presence. I believe that the next wave of Him moving is going to be a holiness wave. We must all deal with our "stuff" on a daily basis so that we walk with integrity. The Holy Spirit is a kind messenger. He is giving us all the opportunity to make wise decisions, to choose forgiveness, and to leave behind our sinful ways at this time. I urge you to let Jesus "dig in the garden of your heart now,"

and to let Him lead you in the process of sanctification and transformation. Choose inner healing daily.

John and I had a friend from England named Terry. When he walked into a room you'd smell English roses very strongly. He wrote out a prophetic word and gave it to me and the paper smelled the same! It was supernaturally covered in oil, so I had to store it in a Ziploc bag. The prophetic word said, "The next wave of my spirit will be birthed out of intimacy. Intimacy can only be found in that secret place where you and I can be as one. Out of this intimacy will come the release of life, power, and fire to enable you to see and feel my glory start to cover the earth. You must find that place, that secret place, that relationship with me." Terry carried that beautiful fragrance of roses with him wherever he went. It was the fragrance of intimacy. After he went to be with Jesus, I found the prophetic word that I'd stored away and the oil was still there, but the smell had gone.

The fragrance that Terry carried was a representation of the beauty of intimacy with the Father. It drew me, and I know many others, into loving Jesus more. We each need to have the fragrance of intimacy in our own lives. It may not be a physical smell, but the intimacy that you have with the Lord will always ooze out and bless those around you.

FILLED TO POUR OUT

If you're not filled with God's presence, your efforts to love and serve other people could become striving, controlling, or manipulative. When you are filled to overflowing with God's presence and when you're being transformed from the inside out, you'll have a better ability to love the people around you. I want to be so filled with His love that I radiate it to everyone I meet.

As you spend time in God's presence, you'll get His heart and see that the lost are really lost. Your perception changes. All of a sudden, you'll find yourself talking to someone at the grocery store when you notice that they are walking with a limp, or you sense that the Holy Spirit is prompting you to ask if their family is okay. You'll find opportunities to pray for people right there. Perhaps, as you soak, the Holy Spirit will put someone on your heart and you'll keep thinking about that person who you haven't thought about in a long time. Write their name down and phone them. When that's

happened to me, it's turned out that a family member has been in the hospital, or they're going through some kind of major struggle. The Holy Spirit knows what everyone is going through and wants to put people on your heart to love them and pray for them.

As you spend time in God's presence, you'll get His Heart and see that the lost are really lost. Your perception changes.

Get yourself in tune with Him and everything else will flow from that place of intimacy and relationship. It's not about striving to do good works, like a servant who says, "Tell me what to do and I'll do it." That servant knows that if they don't obey, there will be punishment. Instead, it's about doing the things He's asked of you from a perspective that you love Him so much. You're working for Him with a focus of pleasing the One you love.

JESUS TAUGHT THE DISCIPLES ABOUT RELATIONSHIP WITH THE FATHER

Jesus so completely loved the Father. He was always talking to the disciples about the Father. They were constantly asking Him questions about what to do, how to live, how to pray and how to love God. In Matthew 6, Jesus taught them the Lord's prayer, about how to talk to their heavenly Father. The beginning of the prayer, *"Our Father in heaven, hallowed be Your name. Your kingdom come. Your will be done on earth as it is in heaven,"* is in the imperative tense. Saying, *"Your kingdom come,"* is less like a request than a command or a declaration. Jesus taught the disciples that prayer is agreeing with what the Father wants, that it is a relational thing. As they hear what He wants, they pray it out. The Father wants us to pray in the same way that Jesus showed the disciples, where we can come boldly before Him, like little children, asking Him what He wants and declaring it back to Him.

Jesus also showed the disciples what a relationship with the Father looks like when they messed up. Peter denied Jesus three times, and I'm sure he thought, "I've blown it so badly that I'm never going to make it. I'm going back to fishing." After Jesus was resurrected, He stood with Peter, eating the fish, and commissioned him three times. He restored Peter's hope and showed him trust and love. Jesus only did what He saw the Father doing and said what He heard the Father saying. Every time Jesus related to the disciples, it was a clear representation of how the Father wants to relate to them, and to us, too. Every time we mess up, the Father is willing to restore us just as Jesus restored Peter.

WHAT DOES A HEALTHY RELATIONSHIP LOOK LIKE?

When we soak, we are spending time intimately building a relationship with God. In a healthy relationship with God, we're always depending on Him. We need to be open for correction from Him along the way, regularly asking, "Do I need to make an adjustment somewhere? Is there something in my heart that I need to deal with?" It's so important to always be on the side of, "I don't have it all together," so that we don't get prideful in our own abilities and become independent from Him.

Every time we mess up, the Father is willing to restore us just as Jesus restored Peter.

The Lord will bring course corrections along the way. Perhaps He'll tell you that it's time to get more inner healing, or to forgive someone. I've had times and seasons when I've focused on Jesus, sometimes with the Holy Spirit, and other times intentionally spending time on the Father's knee, close to Him. I recently realized I needed a season in the Father's house, to spend time with my Heavenly Dad and remember how big He is, how wonderful He is and how much He really loves me. I knew I needed to go deeper in knowing Daddy's great love. Jesus said to His disciples, *"Anyone who has seen me has seen the Father"* (John 14:9 NIV). As you are loving Jesus and building intimacy with Him, He will take you deeper into the Father.

ACTIVATION

What is the focus of your time with God? Is it mostly for yourself? Or is it all about being filled up so you can to pour out to others? Have you spent time lately just loving on Him, for His sake? Tell Him today:

> *Jesus, I just want to tell you I love You. Lord, I want to go deeper with you. Jesus, thank You for everything! Thank You for my breath, thank You for my house, thank You for my family. Lord, I just love You and I just want to spend time with You.*

Then ask Him:

> *What's on Your heart for our relationship? How can I go deeper with You?*

Read John 21. Put yourself in Peter's shoes and imagine how much shame he must have felt after denying Jesus right before His death. Now imagine how much love he must have felt as Jesus rebuilt trust with him. That is the love and compassion that the Father wants to show you when you mess up. Ask God to reveal that love to your heart today.

Chapter 3

THE IMPACT OF SOAKING

FROM SHY TO BOLD IN THE HOLY SPIRIT

I used to be incredibly shy and insecure. I only wanted to stay in the back row, to stay hidden and out of the limelight. Even now, I know that without the Holy Spirit I would be so self-conscious and timid.

When I first married John, he owned a travel agency, but he had previously trained for ministry. Early on in our marriage we took a mission trip to Indonesia and were undone by the love of those people. It was there we realized that we could not give our lives to business. We decided to plant a church in my hometown of Stratford. I used to ask him, "John, what can I do?" I didn't think I had any abilities or talents. I hadn't been to Bible school, I was really afraid to get up in front of people, and I couldn't even do the traditional things that a pastor's wife could do like play the piano! I thought I had nothing. John would simply reply, "Yes, honey, but you can love." I thought that was insignificant; surely everyone could love. I didn't see or appreciate the gifts that God had given me, so I wanted to keep myself hidden, but John kept encouraging me that I had an ability to love the unlovable and that it was a gift from God.

Once a year, John would ask me to speak on the Mother's Day Sunday service. It took me six months to find something to speak on. I spent months searching the Bible for something to say and then the whole night before, I was awake worrying about it. It was awful! I would perspire all the way through the service because I was so nervous about getting up in front of people.

When Marc DuPont first visited our church in Stratford, he prophesied that I'd be preaching to hundreds of pastors and leaders, to thousands of people. I laughed right in His face and said, "Some kind of prophet you are! You are kidding me; you can't be serious!" But God has a way. It wasn't long before the revival began and I started to learn to minister in front of people. I started to soak and to encounter the Holy Spirit, and I discovered His nearness and His love and His absolute delight in me and that built my confidence, bit by bit. Now, I get the opportunity to teach and minister all over the world, sometimes in front of thousands of people. Marc's prophetic word was right. (By the way I've been back and apologized to him since).

The Holy Spirit has made me tenacious.

People laugh at me now when I tell these stories because they don't think I look very shy. The Holy Spirit has made me tenacious. It's not me, it's Him. When the Holy Spirit works in our lives, He brings dramatic transformation. It's been through soaking and marinating in His presence that I've built the boldness and trust in the Lord to go after something when He asks. My whole life changed when I realized that the Lord truly loves me. As I learned to pour out my love on Him and soak in His presence, I received a deep and lasting understanding of His love.

I still don't feel 100 percent confident every time I get up to speak. Recently, I broke my wrist and tore the tendons in my shoulder and arm when I slipped on some ice. I was due to speak at a conference, but I was still in pain and couldn't do everything I was used to doing. I didn't feel as comfortable as I normally would. I had to just take a step back and say, "Lord, I can't do it, but you can." Positioning my heart to know that He's with me and yielding to Him in any moment has become a regular practice for me. I'll tell Him, "Here I am, Lord. Speak through me." When I feel His presence on me, then I know He's with me and I can minister with confidence.

Still, sometimes, God calls us to do something whether we feel His presence or not. We have to rely on faith, not our feelings. I had to learn that in a time of intense sickness. It took me three years of not feeling His presence, which was awful for me. The Lord taught me that He is faithful even in those times when I didn't feel Him and when I didn't have the experience to back up the truth that He is always with me.

SOAKING CHANGES US

When I speak on soaking, I love to use the example of Mr. Sponge. I have a sponge that has a sad, grumpy face drawn onto it. It's dry, crusty, and hard. Mr. Sponge is not a happy sponge. I have a bowl of water on the stage with me and I put Mr. Sponge in there for the duration of the sermon. It always draws a few laughs when, ta-da! Mr. Sponge comes out of the water soaking and dripping wet, with a great big smile on his face. It's a simple and fun example of the change that soaking makes in our lives. It's not easy to forget that image!

I've seen soaking really transform so many people. Heidi Baker has told me many times that she wouldn't be able to do what she does without a consistent soaking life. I have many friends that I call "super soakers" who really invest time in God's presence and Heidi is at the top of that list.

Steve Long, the senior leader of Catch The Fire Church in Toronto, used to find it a little harder to feel the presence of God. In the early days of the revival, we used to say that he was like an oak tree. He never moved or felt anything. So he decided to spend 10 or 15 minutes soaking every night, lying on the floor beside his bed. He wouldn't get in the bed because he didn't want to fall asleep. He would listen to worship music and take time to receive. Months later, a pastor from Ottawa was using the Mr. Sponge example to teach on soaking. He asked for a volunteer to pick up the bowl of water at the end of his message. So Steve jumped up, got on the platform, held the bowl, and as the pastor picked up the soaking wet sponge and squeezed the water out, all of a sudden, Steve fell right back, holding the bowl of water in his hand, not spilling a drop. The Holy Spirit fell on him and he responded dramatically. Nothing like that had happened to him before. God honoured Steve's faithfulness in soaking. Steve chose to soak out of obedience and not by feeling, but now, he can really receive and feel much more of the Holy Spirit than he could before. Soaking dramatically increased his capacity to experience God.

"I ONLY SAY WHAT I HEAR THE FATHER SAYING"

Do you want to learn to experience the reality of God? It's about learning to live in His presence every day. Jesus said that He only did what He saw the Father doing and He only said what He heard the Father saying (see John 5:19). I want to continually remember to pray that prayer. I'm nowhere near doing and saying what the Father is doing and saying all of the time, but can you imagine what would happen if all believers could walk as Jesus walked? What would happen? The blind would see, the deaf

Can you imagine what would happen if all believers could walk as Jesus walked?

would hear, we'd see immediate freedom from sickness and infirmities. It would be incredible! We'd lead people into a relationship with Jesus here, there, and everywhere. I want to be that connected and that close to the Father.

DEVELOPING INTIMACY

Soaking opens up the heart and soul to romance and intimacy with the Lord. It allows the Lord to love you and you to love Him, much like a couple in love find that their love and intimacy deepens as they spend more and more time together. My mother used to say, "For crying out loud, you've been on the phone with John for two hours. And you talked to him yesterday! What do you talk about?"

I'd reply, "I don't know. We just talk. We just want to be together." When you're with somebody that you really love, you just want to spend time with them. It really doesn't matter what you say. It's more about being together, walking together, loving them, and knowing them.

> **Intimacy with the Lord is about connecting with Him all the time.**

You don't have to lie down and soak to experience intimacy. Intimacy with the Lord is about connecting with Him all the time. I love to be out in my garden communing with Him. It's a time to connect my heart with His heart, just to sit together. He just loves that communion and I love it too. He wants to be together in the significant moments and the little day-to-day moments when nobody else is watching.

As I've developed intimacy with the Lord, I've found that He really cares about the little details. I can never find my glasses. I take them off, set them down, and later, when I need them to read something, I can't find them. I'll say, "Father, where did I put my glasses?" and He'll tell me in an instant. It blows my mind that the God of the universe, who has much more to do than to remind me where my glasses are, still wants to be involved in the mundane details. Soaking builds that kind of sweetness in everyday relationship.

LEARNING TO HEAR GOD SPEAK

I love Mark Virkler's teaching on hearing God's voice.[1] In the early days of our church, God spoke clearly to John that there were some important values that we needed at the core of our ministry, including teaching how to hear God's voice. We got connected with Mark Virkler, who had spent a year searching the scriptures for a clear guide to hearing God speak and found four simple keys out of Habakkuk 2:1-2. When someone learns to hear God's voice for themselves, it completely changes their relationship with Him. It becomes living and active.

Many of us hear the devil loud and clear and our own thoughts loud and clear, but don't know how to listen for the still small voice of the Lord, unless we're taught how to. The first key that Mark Virkler teaches is to quiet yourself down. Soaking teaches us to quiet ourselves down to find the gentle voice of God. Of course, He can speak loudly, but most of the time we experience Him in a whisper, like Elijah, rather than in a loud voice. In lives that are so full of busy clatter, quieting ourselves down is really important.

Mark Virkler's second key to hearing God's voice is to fix your eyes on Jesus. Soaking is all about focusing on your Beloved. It's taking your eyes off the rest of life to adore Him and commune with Him. Thirdly, Mark teaches that we must tune to spontaneous thoughts. Soaking helps you learn to hear God through your thoughts and through the eyes of

> **Soaking helps you learn to hear God through your thoughts and through the eyes of your heart.**

your heart. Finally, Mark teaches that we need to write down and record everything that God says, so that we can be accountable with two others as we learn to hear God and so that we have a record to look back on.

So many times I've had people tell me, "I was soaking and I thought about so-and-so, so I made a note and called them later." It turned out that the person was in a crisis or really needed encouragement. That's the voice of God putting that person in their mind. When we understand that God speaks and that often it's in a gentle voice, we're able to honour those little thoughts that come into our minds and we're more likely to do something about it.

Once, I had a man come up to me at a meeting and tell me that he was so frustrated with soaking. He'd been doing it for over a year and every time he lay down to soak, all he'd hear from God was, "I love you, my son." The man asked me, "Doesn't He have anything better to say to me?" He asked me to pray for him. I told him to lie down and soak, asking God why He was doing this, telling Him his frustrations and seeing what God was saying. Well, he lay down for a few minutes and came back to me with tears in his eyes. The Lord had spoken to him clearly: "I'll keep saying it to you until you start to believe it." He was so moved and so encouraged to keep soaking in God's presence.

> Every time you soak, take time to ask Him what He wants to say to you. He's never lost for words toward you.

You need to know that God really loves you. God wants to permeate whatever part of your heart still doesn't believe it. As we learn to hear God in soaking, His truth sinks in deep, right

where we need it. Every time you soak, take time to ask Him what He wants to say to you. He's never lost for words toward you, as it says in Psalm 139:17, *"How precious to me are your thoughts, God! How vast is the sum of them!"* (NIV).

RECEIVING HEALING

Resting in the presence of God heals us. When we soak, God will speak to us and heal us of our past hurts. Sometimes He'll even do things in our hearts and heal us when we didn't know it, just like going under anesthetic for surgery. He is a gentle healer! He wants to deal with the issues of your heart, to bring you peace where there is anxiety, and to bring you comfort where there is pain. In our School of Ministry in Toronto, the students have time allotted in their schedule to soak every week. When this was first implemented, the leaders noticed a dramatic difference in the students' needs for one-on-one ministry and counselling because they were bringing their needs before God and letting Him minister to their hearts.

Resting in the presence of God heals us.

I've also seen many examples of people soaking, or receiving soaking prayer, and then receive physical healing. You can read some amazing examples in chapter eight where, people have been dramatically healed through soaking.

DREAMS, AND VISIONS, SIGNS AND WONDERS

The anointing of God's presence increases as you spend quality time with Jesus. I've seen people strive to attain the supernatural in their ministry, but it's so much better to allow God to move through you when it's from a place of rest.

Dreams and Visions

Before I started soaking I never had a vision. I also believed that I didn't dream. Then I realized that God loves to speak to people through dreams. I quickly repented and asked God to speak to me through dreams and visions.

Just as Mark Virkler teaches, we must allow God to speak to us through pictures. God wants to use the eyes of your heart. Dreams and visions are a really important part of the way that God wants to speak to us. We see them all throughout the Bible. One of my favorites is Joseph. God spoke to Joseph in dreams and he had to learn how to use this gift. Eventually, his ability to interpret Pharaoh's dreams saved a nation from famine.

Three weeks into the revival in 1994, not long after I'd repented of believing that I couldn't see visions or dream dreams, I had a long 45-minute open vision in technicolor about the bride and the bridegroom that totally deepened my awareness of spiritual realities. All of a sudden, I could see for myself that God can give us visions and dreams. It was amazing.

Sometimes, when I'm soaking, I'll ask the Lord if He has anything to show me, or anywhere He wants to take me. Often, He'll show me a picture of me walking with Jesus beside a beautiful river with a big oak tree beside it. It's bright aqua blue, reminding me of the rivers in British Columbia, Canada. In the vision, there's a meadow beside the river. Jesus and I will just talk. It's such a peaceful, restful place, away from the hustle and bustle of daily life.

I grew up believing that I couldn't see in the Spirit, but I'm so grateful that it's possible for all of us to see and hear God through dreams and visions. I wouldn't say I dream a lot, but when I do, they're usually pretty profound. God has spoken to me with warnings and with blueprints and plans in dreams that have affected the direction of my life.

It's possible for all of us to hear God through dreams and visions.

Signs and Wonders

Many of us are hungry to see signs, wonders, and miracles happen in and through our lives. This is such a wonderful thing to pursue, but it must always come from intimacy and relationship. Otherwise, pride will always get in the way. Through soaking, you learn that God is really present. You immerse yourself and know that He wants to spend time with you. If we want to see miracles, signs, and wonders, we must listen to what God wants to do, just as Jesus said and did what He heard and saw the Father saying and doing.

With miracles, you're always walking on the water. It's about trust—putting your hand in His hand, knowing that Jesus paid the price for people to be healed. Miracles don't always happen in the way that we expect. Sometimes healing happens more slowly than we would hope, but God is always the healer. We must always trust that when He directs us to do something, that's because He wants to move in people's lives.

I'm still very much learning how to hold Jesus' hand and trust Him to see miracles happen. I know that every meeting that I minister in is a training ground. In 2017, I was in England at our Revival Alliance conference. We were doing two conferences back to back, one in Tonsberg, Norway and one in Birmingham, England. John's plane was late arriving from Norway and he was due to be teaching a morning session. Lori, our daughter, asked if I could facilitate people giving testimonies while we waited for John to arrive. The night before, Bill Johnson had taught. At the end, he had given a call for healing, with some words of knowledge.

With miracles, you're always walking on the water. It's about trust—putting your hand in His hand, knowing that Jesus paid the price for people to be healed.

I got up on the platform and invited people up to give testimonies from the night before. Lori met a woman at the side of the stage who had got out of her wheelchair the night before, but she wasn't walking very well. She asked me if I wanted to invite her up to testify, even though she hadn't received her full healing yet. I said, "Of course, God's doing something in her. Let's corporately pray for her."

Soaking people in prayer will very often facilitate greater healing. A lot of times, when John does a call for ministry and someone is not quite fully healed, maybe they're 70% percent better or so, I'll spend five or ten minutes with them. We've discovered that many times there is a forgiveness issue, or trauma, or words spoken over the person by a doctor that is blocking their full healing. Taking a few minutes to pray through forgiveness and repentance often brings greater breakthrough.

We brought the lady up to the front of the meeting. I helped her forgive and repent for the areas that God was leading us into, and then as a whole room, we started to believe and pray together for her complete healing. I started walking her back and forth across the stage, which was a fairly large stage, and after a few times back and forth, she was walking, completely normal!

Soaking people in prayer will very often facilitate greater healing.

While I was with this lady, I had a word of knowledge. Sometimes God speaks to me through symptoms in my own body, which is harder to discern the older you get because there's always a little pain somewhere! This time, I had a sharp pain like glass shards going down my legs. I had no idea what it was, so I explained on the microphone what I was feeling and that I thought it was because God wanted to heal somebody. All of a sudden, a lady got up from her chair and started screaming. Lori brought her up to the stage and she explained that she had cancer, and every time she had chemotherapy, she had pain in her legs which felt like glass shards in her veins. The instant that I announced what I was feeling, all the pain left her body. It was totally God!

Then, out of my mouth came, "I want everyone in wheelchairs in this place to come up. God is going to heal you." Immediately I wanted to take the words back! The meeting room was huge and I had no idea how many wheelchairs there might be! I knew I couldn't do a single thing to help them in my own strength. I asked the Lord, "Oh God, what did I just say?" I put my hand up to my chest and touched a little heart necklace that Beni Johnson had given me. Inscribed on the heart is, "God's got this." I said to Him, "God, I don't have this. Do you have this?" And He said, "I have it, Carol." I knew that if He had it, I could go for it. I felt like I was walking on water. Together with everyone in the room, we prayed for all of the people who came up in wheelchairs and saw everyone who had been in a wheelchair walking! Some incredible breakthrough!

In that kind of situation, you need to know that God is with you. You need to have practiced that intimate communication already so that you know you can trust Him. If He asks you to do something, or you find yourself in a situation ministering to someone and you have no faith, simply tell Him, "God, I'm really scared. I don't know what to do." Then, step back into His presence. Find out how He wants to order the battle. Ask Him what His plans are.

It's all about communication and about knowing Him. When best friends spend a lot of time together, they begin to really know each other's hearts. They know the intonation of the other's voice if they're struggling that day and they're trying to put on a good face. Have you seen how some best friends even start to dress similarly? They have similar tastes and things that they enjoy together. That comes with spending time together. It's the same with Jesus—the more time we spend with Him, the more we know Him and the safer and more trust-filled our communication with Him becomes.

> When best friends spend a lot of time together, they begin to really know each other's hearts. It's the same with Jesus—the more time we spend with Him, the more we know Him and the safer and more trust-filled our communication with Him becomes.

EFFECTIVE LEADERSHIP

We all must spend time soaking in the presence of God. Especially if we want to be effective leaders. So many leaders are too busy. They're focused on ministry, like Martha. Many leaders read the Word and pray, but they're striving rather than resting. The most effective leadership comes out of a relationship of resting in the affection of the Father, not striving, working, or doing to earn His love.

ACTIVATION

As you soak, make space for God to speak to you. Follow Mark Virkler's keys to hear His voice—quiet yourself down, fix your eyes on Jesus, tune in to spontaneous thoughts, and write down what He says. Start by asking, "Lord, what do You want to say to me today? How do You see me?"

NOTE

1. Mark Virkler, "4 Keys to Hearing God," Communion with God Ministries, accessed June 30, 2019, https://www .cwgministries.org/Four-Keys-to-Hearing-Gods-Voice.

Chapter 4

SOAKING THROUGHOUT HISTORY

My Journey into Soaking

When I was first saved, I went to a Kathryn Kuhlman meeting. When she prayed for me, I fell down. I got so overwhelmed by God's power but I didn't stay on the floor for too long. Years later, after John and I were married, we would go to Benny Hinn meetings. He and John knew each other since they were young and the Lord was moving powerfully in Benny's ministry. We loved going to see and experience what God was doing through Benny. In one meeting, when Benny prayed for me, I got stuck to the floor. I couldn't move, and the longer I stayed there, the more I was overwhelmed by the Holy Spirit. I thought I was going to explode! The feeling on my hands was so intense that it felt like they were 10 times bigger than normal. I didn't know whether I could stand it, but I knew that I loved it.

As time went on, John and I became increasingly hungry for more of God's presence. We wanted to see Him move in a powerful way in our lives and in our church. When we sought Him, God told us to give Him our mornings. In an act of faith, we cancelled all our morning appointments just to be with Him. Every morning we'd spend our time in prayer, in the Word, and in His presence. It was such a joy to intentionally carve out that time for the Lord. Some mornings were filled with intimacy, some were full of new revelation. On other mornings, nothing seemed to happen at all, but we kept going because obedience to God's call was so important to us.

The Lord also told us to go to places where He was moving. When we found out that the Holy Spirit breaking out in Argentina, we knew we had to go. We didn't have the money for a plane ticket; we scraped together, what we had and our

daughter Lori gave us some money even though she couldn't afford it either. We bought plane tickets to go to Buenos Aires in November 1993, believing for an encounter with God. Claudio Friedzon prayed for us while we were there and we were mightily impacted. I was so filled with God's presence again

God told us to give Him our mornings.

that I couldn't get up off the floor and I was soaking in it for hours after. That experience completely changed my life.

Two months after we got home, the Holy Spirit broke out in our own church near the Toronto Airport. It was, beyond anything we could have asked or imagined. One night, while Randy Clark was preaching, the Holy Spirit, came and almost everyone in the room fell to the ground. It seemed to accelerate from there. We started to hold nightly meetings where God would move in incredible ways. We had to walk hand in hand with the Lord because we didn't know what would happen from one meeting to the next. People were mightily impacted by the presence of God. They were falling out under the power of the Holy Spirit and manifesting in ways we could have never imagined.

I got really hit by His presence again. In every meeting, when the presence would fall, I couldn't stand up. Not long after it all started, Marc Dupont, who had prophesied an outpouring of the Holy Spirit in our church, was at a meeting. He asked me, "Carol, how are you going to lead this if you're on the floor?" I was so super sensitive to the Holy Spirit that if anything happened I would be rendered physically incapable of anything but laying in His presence. About two weeks later, he put his hand on my head and said, "Carol, thus says the Lord, you can stand or you can yield." That was a wake-up call for me. I had to actually learn to stand under the anointing and minister. Even then, many people would pray for me during meetings to try and get me to fall down. I so loved spending time receiving, but I had to learn to stand up so that I could minister to other people as well.

> They were falling out under the power of the Holy Spirit and manifesting in ways we could have never imagined.

ON THE PRAYER LINES

The more I received God's presence, the more I soaked Him in, the more fruit I saw in my life. I became more full of the Holy Spirit and fell more in love with Jesus. It wasn't long before John and I noticed the same thing happening on the prayer lines too. The ministry team would pray for everyone who came to a meeting and many of them fell down under the Holy Spirit's power. Those who took time to stay on the floor and receive, came away so transformed. We started to encourage people to stay and rest and wait on the floor because we saw such good results. People had incredible encounters with the Father, Son, and Holy Spirit; hearts were healed, marriages were restored, and people received vision and direction.

We started to call this process of abiding in the presence "soaking." We got the name from Francis MacNutt who taught on soaking people in prayer for healing.[1] Just as you would soak or rest in a warm bath and your whole body becomes warm, he taught that as we pray for people over long periods of time, it was like the prayer and presence of God would warm their bodies and he'd see increased levels of physical healing. I'd already been spending time pursuing an intimate love affair with the Lord but learning about Francis MacNutt's ministry confirmed to me that the Lord loves for us to tarry in His presence.

At this time, I also learned that staying and waiting with someone after they received prayer was really impactful. Each night, we would call people up to the front and pray for them before the message, such as pastors and leaders, or people from specific countries. The Lord would pinpoint someone to me, and I would soak them in prayer at the front.

In the beginning, that's all I thought I could do, because I couldn't speak confidently and I didn't feel like I was anointed. But I said yes to what the Lord was calling me to do. He'd highlight someone, usually after they fell down in His presence, and I'd pray for them for as long as I felt the Lord instructed. Sometimes it would be half an hour, sometimes it would be just 10 minutes. Sometimes it would be for hours. Some people would open their eyes and be ready to get up after a few minutes, but I'd always tell them to keep waiting on the Lord. One of those people was Michael Brodeur, who was pastoring a Vineyard church at the time. I soaked him in prayer for four hours! Now, over 20 years later, Michael has been incredibly helpful and influential for our movement as we plant more churches. I also prayed for revival leaders like Ché Ahn, Georgian and Winnie Banov, Bill and Beni Johnson, and Heidi Baker before their ministries really launched. What an honour to partner with God as He ministered to them.

People had incredible encounters with the Father, Son, and Holy Spirit; hearts were healed, marriages were restored, and people received vision and direction.

SOAKING ISN'T SOMETHING NEW

Soaking isn't just a good idea that turned up in the '90s in Toronto. Believers have been marinating in God's presence for centuries but just calling it by different names. There are accounts throughout history of Christians resting, abiding, and tarrying in the presence of God.

Just a few hundred years after Jesus walked the earth, there was a movement called the Desert Fathers.[2] They lived

in the desert in Egypt, to pursue a more pure Christian life. One of their values was spending time in rest and quiet. They would pray and wait on God in silence. They knew that you couldn't strive to make something happen. They knew the importance of meditation—connecting with God's heart and hearing what He has to say.

> The Desert Fathers knew the importance of meditation—connecting with God's heart and hearing what He has to say.

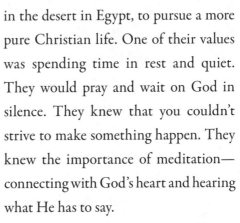

In the 1730s, God poured out His presence across America in the great awakening. Jonathan Edwards was very influential in the Great Awakening and his wife Sarah, talked about her own radical encounters with God:

> But all night I continued in a constant, clear and lively sense of the heavenly sweetness of Christ's excellent and transcendent love, of His nearness to me, and of my dearness to Him; with an inexpressibly sweet calmness of soul in an entire rest in Him. I seemed to myself to perceive a glow of divine love come down from the

heart of Christ in heaven, into my heart, in a constant stream, like a stream or pencil of sweet light. At the same time, my heart and soul all flowed out in love to Christ, so that there seemed to be a constant flowing and reflowing of heavenly and divine love, from Christ's heart to mine; and I appeared to myself to float or swim, in these bright, sweet beams of the love of Christ, His light like the motes swimming in the beams of the sun, or the streams of His light which come in at the window.[3]

This sounds a lot like my own experiences of soaking! I love the way she talks about, "His nearness to me, and...my dearness to Him," This is such a beautiful description of the intimacy that we can experience with the Lord when we soak.

Smith Wigglesworth, a powerful preacher and healing minister in England in the early 1900s, talked a lot about abiding in God's presence. In one of his sermons he said:

If you are in His love, you will be swallowed up with holy desire. You will have no desire, only the Lord. Your mind will be filled with divine reflection. Your whole heart will be taken up with things that pertain to the Kingdom of God, and you will live in the secret place of the Most High, and you will abide there. Remember, it is abiding where He covers you with His feathers. It is an inner, inner, inner, inner place where the Lord now has the treasures.[4]

This also sounds so much like soaking to me. It's that inner secret place where we abide with God. Wigglesworth was constantly in the Word, letting it permeate him and soaking in the truth, like the Desert Fathers.

A few years ago, John and I visited a small church in Sunderland, where God moved powerfully and the Pentecostal movement was born in Britain. I've heard that they would talk about *"tarrying until the glory comes down"* just like the disciples were instructed to in Luke 24. There were indentations on the walls where they stacked slabs up on the walls. When people fell out under the power of the presence of God, they'd put them on one of these slabs and let them tarry and rest in God's presence. I found it funny just thinking of all these people on slabs. Can you imagine realizing that you'd been put on one of the top slabs? What would happen when they wanted to get down? It's just the same kind of thing that started happening in our church in 1994. People would fall down and we'd let them rest and wait and receive from God as long as they wanted. Thankfully we had enough room on the carpet that we didn't have to stack them in specially made shelves on the walls!

SOAKING DURING THE LAST 25 YEARS

Since the revival began, soaking has become a huge part of my life. The way it looks has changed through different seasons, but it's always been about developing intimacy with the Holy Spirit. I have a friend in England and we used to soak together over Skype. We would soak for two hours or longer! We'd both experience God doing the same thing as we spent time with the Lord "together," even though we were so far apart.

Our team in Toronto trained leaders to open soaking centres all around the world. They were places where people could gather together, outside of a regular church meeting, just to soak together. Just to spend time adoring Jesus and resting in His presence. People were soaking in groups in their living rooms, basements, and churches, all over the world!

In life, it's normal that your focus changes with different seasons. I had a really deep season in the wilderness with one sickness after the other for about three years. I would soak, but I just couldn't feel the presence of God like I did before. I knew of course that He was there, but I wasn't experiencing Him like I used to. At that time, I heard about Dr. Arne Elsen from Germany, a medical doctor who got saved and started to read two pages of the Bible each day and to use a timer to worship every 10 minutes.[5] He decided to encourage his patients to use a timer that would go off every 10 minutes, to remind them to worship and pray. He saw a dramatic number of physical healings for cancer patients and other people with terminal illnesses. I started using a timer and it really got me back on track. It was hard at first, but slowly I began to know the Holy Spirit experientially again.

The timer focused me on the goodness of God. Somebody would cut me off in traffic and I would have been just about to say something negative and the buzzer would go off. James 3:10 says that you can't curse and bless God at the same time.

I saw how true that was. You can't be negative or irritated and praise God at the same time.

In life, it's normal that your focus changes with different seasons.

The timer got me back to basics. It got me back into worshipping God and focusing back on His goodness and kindness. I realized once again that spending that time in His presence really isn't a waste of time. Soaking is always worth

it! Just like Mary, who chose to spend time with Jesus rather than keeping up with all the things to do. Mary was proactive and Jesus said to Martha, *"it will not be taken away from her."* (Luke 10:42 NIV). I knew I needed to become proactive about being with Jesus once again.

SOAKING AND MEDITATION: WHAT'S THE DIFFERENCE?

Spending time meditating on Jesus and meditating in the Word has continued to become more popular over the last decade. I recently began exploring Lectio Divina, where you take a scripture, read it through very slowly, and ask the Holy Spirit to speak to you through it.[6] It's a beautiful combination of the Word and the Spirit and it's opened up a whole new way of hearing God speak and letting scripture resonate in my heart and life.

In my opinion, meditating on the Word is really important, but it's a whole different thing to soaking simply for a love affair with Jesus, where you have no agenda. Where you take time to say, "Jesus, I position myself to hear what you want to say to me." Of course, sometimes when you soak, God may lead you to a scripture to focus on and meditate on, but it's about letting Him lead as He wants to.

"Jesus, I position myself to hear what you want to say to me."

ACTIVATION

Have you made time recently to rest in the presence of God? It's easy to get caught up in the busyness of life, but the Desert Fathers and many believers throughout history teach us that it's always worthwhile to spend time waiting on the Holy Spirit. Make space this week to soak. Simply make a quiet space, turn on some music, and welcome the Holy Spirit. Make this your prayer:

> *I just love you, Lord. I dust off all the busyness of today and this week. Lord, I want to know your heart. You say that if we ask, you will answer. So Lord, I ask today that you would come, that you*

would fill me, that you would allow me to love
you and let you love me.

NOTES

1. Francis MacNutt, *The Prayer That Heals* (Notre Dame, IN: Ave Maria Press, 2005).

2. Unknown Author, "Desert Fathers," Wikipedia, retrieved from https://en.wikipedia.org/wiki/Desert_Fathers on 2019, May 18.

3. Sarah Pierrepont Edwards, qtd. in Sereno E. Dwight, *Sereno, D. E. (1830), The Life of President Edwards: With a Memoir of His Life* (New York: G. & C. & H. Carvill, 1830), pp. 171-190, retrieved from https://digital.library.upenn.edu/women/pierrepont/conversion/conversion.html.

4. Smith Wigglesworth, S. (2013), *Manifesting the Divine Nature: Abiding In Power Every Day of the Year* (Shippensburg, PA: Destiny Image, 2013), P.71.

5. Catch The Fire Toronto, "Dr. Arne Elsen (30 October 2011) Family Meeting," YouTube, September 19, 2012, retrieved from https://www.youtube.com/watch?v=Z51CfmooIDE, 1:22:30 onward.

6. Unknown Author, "Worship Information Sheet: Lectio Divina," Anglican Communion, https://www.anglicancommunion.org/media/253799/1-What-is-Lectio-Divina.pdf on 2019, May 18.

Chapter 5

SERVANTS AND LOVERS

A RESTLESS CULTURE

I've met many people who can't rest in God's presence. They must constantly be "on duty," accomplishing things, finishing tasks and doing things all the time.

You probably grew up in a culture that values your productivity so highly that time to rest gets put to one side. We get taught from early childhood that how well we perform equates to how successful we are. Your teachers may have told you, "Stop daydreaming and get on with your work." Your parents may have only praised you when you got good grades or worked hard to accomplish something. Those words and actions have a big effect on how we live our adult lives and how we relate to God. We fall into the trap of believing that life with God is about fulfilling tasks and getting things done in order to be successful or be loved by Him.

Our cities, churches, jobs, and homes are full of busyness. There are so many good and valuable things that we can do with our time that it's easy to overcommit. We replace our time for rest and connection, with action and productivity. Life can't go on like that for very long before you get tired and burnt out. Our immediate problems become so overwhelming that we lose sight of Jesus, our first love.

When we started our church in Stratford, I quickly got busy doing lots of things that I thought were good. I spent time listening to people, helping them with their problems, and taking care of church activities. If somebody said to me, "Carol, you've lost your first love." I would have laughed at

them and said, "Of course I haven't!" But that's exactly what had happened. I had gotten so distracted from dealing with people's problems and the challenges of life that I had forgotten how wonderfully big and awesome God really is.

> We replace our time for rest and connection with action and productivity. Life can't go on like that for very long before you get tired and burnt out.

Scripture says, *"Be still, and know that I am God"* (Psalm, 46:10). It doesn't say, "Accomplish a lot and know that I am God." God is calling us to be still and acknowledge Him, to remember that He is big and He is in control. He is calling us to rest in Him. We are human beings, not human doings. He wants us to spend time just being with Him, not always doing things for Him.

A lot of us will let the Lord love us when we feel like we deserve it, if we've really been praying, reading the Bible, and serving Him. If we've been too busy for those things, we feel like we haven't earned His love. We forget that Jesus paid the ultimate price for us to have a relationship with the Father. God really wants to have a relationship with us and we need to accept this love. God is love and He wants us to be lovers.

CHANGING YOUR CULTURE

As we grow up, we adopt the culture that surrounds us without even noticing. Culture is defined as, "The characteristic features of everyday experience shared by people in a place or time."[1] We learn habits, attitudes, and beliefs from our parents, friends, and teachers. As we move into adulthood, we can choose to change the culture that we want to adopt. That includes the culture of busyness. We can choose to create a value for rest and connection with God over and above the desire to be productive. The Bible has lots to say about good works and good stewardship, which are to follow us. But we are talking here about motivation of the heart. You want to serve Him rather than gain approval.

> As we move into adulthood, we can choose to change the culture that we want to adopt.

When we make time to soak, we rest in God's presence and remind ourselves that it's so important to be still and know that His love for us is deep and fulfilling. Of course, soaking doesn't mean that you're not going to accomplish anything or that we're going to give up on all the good things that we do and become lazy. True fruitfulness comes from intimacy with the Lord. As we spend time with Him, we understand His heart and learn to hear His word and how He wants us to spend our time each day. From that place, He directs our hearts to the things that He wants us to be doing. We can use up so much energy trying to accomplish things, but if it's not what the Lord is asking, it's not going to be worthwhile. As, it says in First Corinthians 13, we can do all sorts of good things, but without love, it's worth nothing.

We can do all sorts of good things, but without love, it's worth nothing.

John and I minister at a lot of conferences. When we're at our home church and we know the team well, I'll stop the organizers as they're running around. A conference is a demanding job; the staff are full-on for a whole week at a time. I love to pray for them and to encourage them to just pause, take a minute, and have a drink of the Holy Spirit. It only takes a moment to receive more from Him so that they can get up and go again, in His strength rather than their own.

I HAVE MANY SERVANTS BUT FEW LOVERS

God spoke to me and said, "I have many servants but few lovers." What do you want to be? Do you have the attitude of a servant of God or a lover of God? Jesus said that the most important thing you can do is love Him with all your heart and your soul and to love your neighbour, as yourself (see Mark 12:29-31).

Before John and I were married, we were spending time together and he asked me to make him a cup of tea. I got up straightaway and his mom said, "Oh, for heaven's sake, Carol. He's quite capable of making it himself." But I replied, "I love him. I would love to make a cup of tea!" I didn't feel forced into making the cup of tea, or that I had to make it for John to be pleased with me; I just wanted to do it for him out of love.

That's the attitude that we're called to have as lovers of God. Lovers do things for Him out of a heart of love, to please Him and just to love Him. Servants work for God, thinking, "I'm expected to do this, and if I don't do it, then I'm going to get bad marks. God the Father's going to get upset with me and there's probably punishment down the road." Perhaps your thinking isn't as obvious as this, but if you're stuck in a cycle of work, work, work and you struggle to rest, then you'll probably have that attitude toward God, too.

There is so much need in the world, but if we don't have a love affair with the Lord first, then what are we giving those around us?

It's true that the lost are really lost, the hurting are really hurting, and the hungry are really hungry. There is so much need in the world, but if we don't have a love affair with the Lord first, then what are we giving those around us? We're not going to reflect and represent God's love in an authentic way.

Martha and Mary are a perfect model of a servant and a lover. In Luke 10, we read their story. Can you imagine being in their home? Here's how I picture it: All of a sudden, Martha has got 13 people to feed. Martha was probably a good cook; she's starting to get things ready and then she looks around and sees that Mary isn't there to help her. Mary is at the feet of Jesus, just looking at Him, drawing in His love. Martha gets so perturbed, she's absolutely fit to be tied. She calls Mary over, "Psst, Mary, come here," but to no response. Finally, she can't stand it anymore and she walks up to Jesus and accuses, "Do you not care that my sister has left me to do all the work?" Jesus replies, "Martha, you are so troubled and so worried about many things. But one thing is needed and that will not be taken away from her. Mary has chosen the best."

It's there in the Bible for all of us to see. The best is being with Jesus, just sitting in His presence. Mary valued time with Jesus, whereas Martha was serving and working and Jesus rebuked her.

You might argue that it was easier for Mary to spend time with Jesus, because His physical presence was in the room. But we have the Holy Spirit, who is ever present with us.

The most valuable thing we have to give is our time. Matthew 6:21 says, *"Where your treasure is, there your heart will be also."* The way you use your time will always show what's most important to you. The enemy of our souls, satan, wants to rob us of the time just to love Jesus and to let Him love on us. God wants us to take time in His presence and not to be in a hurry. So what if you miss supper, or don't get your house clean this week? It won't kill you!

TRANSFORMED INTO HIS LIKENESS

I really believe that soaking is a major key to becoming more like Jesus. The more time you spend with Him, the more you'll get to know who He is, what He loves, and what He wants. In Exodus 34, we see that Moses spent time in the presence of God and his face shone:

> *So he was there with the Lord forty days and forty nights; he neither ate bread nor drank water. And He wrote on the tablets the words of the covenant, the Ten Commandments. Now it was so, when Moses came down from Mount Sinai (and the two tablets of the Testimony were in Moses' hand when he came down from the mountain), that Moses did not know that the skin of his face shone while he talked with Him. So when Aaron and all the children of Israel saw Moses, behold, the skin of his face shone, and they were afraid to come near him* (Exodus 34:28-30).

He was immersed so deeply in God's presence that His spirit, soul, and body was infused with the glory of God. He was radiating God's glory.

I've seen a glimpse of people radiating God's glory. Sometimes I've looked at Heidi Baker and she is glowing because she is radiating the presence of God. People have said that about John, and others as well. I don't think I've seen anything close to Moses, but wouldn't it be incredible to be so filled with the glory of God that you shone? I would love to see that. It comes at the cost of spending that time with Him.

> Wouldn't it be incredible to be so filled with the Glory of God that you shone?

THE BRIDE AND THE BRIDEGROOM

Another beautiful picture of intimacy with God is the bride and the bridegroom. It is the divine romance between Jesus and His church. Ephesians 5:27 talks about us becoming the Bride of Christ, *"that He might present her to Himself a glorious church, not having spot or wrinkle or any such thing, but that she should be holy and without blemish."*

Jesus is looking for your love. He is looking for a bride who loves Him. Jesus is coming back for a bride who is compatible and comparable to Him. For the bride to be pleasing to the glorious Bridegroom, she must be glorious too. As a church, we become more glorious as we are immersed in God's presence, saturated and overflowing with love for Him and love for one another.

Three weeks into the revival in 1994, John and I were due to go on a trip to Hungary. We were trying so hard to get out of it because the revival of a lifetime was going on in our church. We couldn't change or cancel the plans, so we went. The church prayed for us and blessed us before the trip. That night I had the most amazing vision that made me understand the divine romance between Jesus and His church.

I had never had a vision ever in my life before then. John would say to me, "Close your eyes and picture your house." I would close my eyes and it would just be black. I could tell you what my house looked like, but I couldn't see it. Marc DuPont was speaking that night, and as he prayed for me I instantly went into an incredible technicolor vision. I was standing in a beautiful meadow and Jesus walked up to me, handing me a bouquet of lily of the valley.

Straightaway that meant so much to me. Years before that vision, I had been going through a really rough time. At that time my divorce was finally over and I had met John. One day, I was driving home from a nearby town, with a bouquet of lilies of the valley that John and his mom had sent me sitting in the car beside me. I was feeling so sorry for myself, wondering what to do about all the things that were going on in my life. As I was thinking and talking to God, the smell of the lilies came up toward my nose. I picked up the bouquet and the Lord spoke to me. He said, "Carol, the lily of the valley is a very tiny and very fragrant flower and it does not grow on the mountaintops, it only grows in the valleys. I'll always have my lilies there for you when you're in a valley."

So in the vision when Jesus handed me a bouquet of lily of the valley, I knew exactly what He meant. He was showing me His closeness and kindness even when I was in a "valley" or hard time. Jesus and I ran through the meadow that was filled with flowers. We laughed and we talked about our past times together in prayer. It was such a precious time.

Then Jesus came up to me and said, "Can I have the bouquet back?" I wasn't too keen on giving back such a special gift, but I handed it to Him anyway. He began to gather together all different colours and varieties of flowers and started to weave them into a circular wreath. He then took the lily of the valley and placed it into the wreath. He put it on my head and out of nowhere came this long white wedding veil. He attached it to the back of the wreath of flowers and instantly the scene changed and I knew that I had my arm over His and we were walking down the street. I had no idea where we were or what was going on. There were people along the way cheering and waving. I looked down and realized, "Oh my gosh, we're walking on the streets of gold. I'm marrying Jesus. Wow!" I felt such excitement and exhilaration.

As soon as I had that thought, the scene changed again. I was in a massive banquet hall. I couldn't see the end of it. All the tables were set with tablecloths, candelabras, and floral arrangements. Everything was ready to go. I realized I'd been invited to the banquet feast of the Lamb. It was so exciting. Then I saw that the room was empty and asked, "Jesus, where is everybody?" I felt to turn around and look behind me and there were all these beautiful people with incredible shining faces and gorgeous wedding attire on. I said, "Lord, who are these people?" He said, "They're the broken, the hurting, the outcasts, the ones who nobody's loved and the ones who nobody's cared for and I have bidden them to come into my banquet feast." Then Jesus walked up to me and He said, "Carol, can I have the first dance now?"

That question was so significant for my heart. Not long after I was saved, I read one morning in Revelation about when we get to heaven and we can lay our crowns before the Lord. I thought, "Lord I don't care about crowns. As a single mom, I just want a hug." I said to Him, "Lord, when I get to heaven, can I just have a really strong long hug from you?" Once I matured as a Christian I understood better what those crowns represent, such as honour and authority,[2]

"...but I have bidden them to come into my banquet feast."

but back then I didn't care about a crown; I just wanted a hug. So in the vision when Jesus came up to me and asked me for the first dance, it was like an answer to my desire from so many years before. Dancing with Jesus and having Him hold me was an answer to that longing in my heart.

Just as we began to dance, I thought, "Oh no! I can't dance with Jesus, my wedding veil is too long!" It was a silly thought, but instantly all these little birds came, cardinals and sparrows and blue jays, and they picked up my wedding veil as I danced with Jesus.

When I came out of the vision, I saw that I was still lying on the floor of the stage, right where Marc DuPont had been preaching. I had been there for 45 minutes. I had been lying on my back and occasionally my feet would come up in the air like I was running and my hands were waving around. I had no idea that I was doing that!

> "Don't touch her. I don't know what's going on, but she would never do this for a million dollars. Something powerful is going on here; leave her alone."

I was quite a distraction to the congregation. John told me afterwards that people kept coming up to him asking to move me away because Marc was speaking. John just said, "Don't touch her. I don't know what's going on, but she would never do this for a million dollars. Something powerful is going on here; leave her alone."

When the vision ended, John got me up and asked me to share what had happened to me. I asked the Lord what He wanted me to share and He asked me to get Jeremy Sinnott, our worship leader, to sing Kevin Prosch's song, "So Come":[3]

You have taken the precious
From the worthless and given us
Beauty for ashes, love for hate
You have chosen the weak things
Of the world to shame that which is strong
And foolish things to shame the wise [3]

After Jeremy sang that song, the Lord said to me, "Tell my people that this is a time where I'm pouring out the oil of my Spirit and they are to be like the five wise virgins in Matthew 25. They all were looking for the soon coming of the Lord. They all carried lamps. They all had them lit. They all slumbered and slept. But what was the difference between the five wise and the five foolish? The five wise had extra oil." He said, "This is a time where I am pouring out the oil of my Spirit. It's going to cost them to buy oil and have extra oil and the cost is vulnerability, humility and pressing into intimacy." I shared what I heard God say and shared the vision with them.

That vision called me into intimacy and a passion for Jesus. It showed me that He wants to give His Bride eyes only for Him. The Lord loves intimacy. He wants closeness with each one of us. He wants to spend time with us and to show us the things of His heart. It also revealed to John and me the importance of manifestations of God's presence. We learned how important it is not to interfere with what God is intending to do in that person. We need to stay in tune with what God is saying in the moment and follow His lead. A couple of years later, John was reading Matthew 25 over and over again. He kept rereading the scripture to glean more truth that the Lord wanted to show us. The Lord revealed to him that the vision was a prophetic overview of what He was doing in Toronto. The Lord was painting a blueprint of this vision on my heart, which we now know was prophetic symbolism. The Lord spoke to John and said, "if you had stopped Carol to preserve her dignity, or yield to the pressure from the people, or for the sake of tidying up the meeting, the revival would have lasted about three weeks." Why? We would have been stopping the prophetic process that the Holy Spirit was doing as He was painting a divine blueprint on my heart. Toronto became a place where the nations came to buy the oil of the Holy Spirit. We've been amazed as over the years God continues to move mightily. What a privilege it is to get to be part of a revival that continues on and on, and that has impacted people all over the earth!

I didn't expect that I could have a vision like that before it happened. God opened the eyes of my heart and He wants

When the Lord speaks, grab on to it and pursue what He's saying through it.

to open yours too. He wants to give you a closer, more intimate walk with Him, where He can reveal Himself to you in new ways. Most people, including me, don't get those kinds of wild technicolor visions all the time. Sometimes it's like the old-fashioned negatives on a film. Sometimes it's dull and you just get a glimpse of something that the Lord is revealing to you. Sometimes your mind will kick in and tell you it's just you, but when the Lord speaks that way, grab on to it and pursue what He's saying through it.

For a while after I had that bridal vision, I thought that I had to wait for a sovereign encounter with the Lord to see what He was showing me in a vision. I had to learn that I can position myself to hear what God is saying and to see what He's doing. Sometimes God will initiate, but He also wants us to ask Him questions. It's that two-way love affair, where we pursue knowing the things of His heart, at the same time He pursues us and speaks to us.

ACTIVATION

What is your culture like? Did you grow up with teachers and family members teaching you that it's far more valuable to work hard and get things done than to take time to rest? As a child did you have to achieve certain things at school in order to gain approval from your parents and feel loved by others? If so, that's probably affected how you view God—you feel like you need to work hard to please Him and be loved by Him.

Take time to forgive anyone in your life who may have taught you that you need to work hard or perform well in order to be loved.

Father, I was taught by (insert people's names) that I had to work hard to be loved and that made me believe that you want me to strive for Your love too. I understand that You don't operate like that, that You ask me to rest and receive Your love rather than striving to be loved by You. I choose to forgive everyone who influenced me to think that way. Help me to know in my heart that You love me just as I am, before I do anything.

In the next few days, examine your thinking. Are you critical of yourself when you don't complete the plans you had for that day? Do you set your standards really high for what you must do and how well you must do it? As each negative thought comes into your mind, take it captive. Ask the Lord for His thoughts toward you in that moment. He loves you unconditionally.

NOTES

1. *Merriam-Webster Dictionary*, s.v. "Culture," accessed June 14, 2019, https://www.merriam-webster.com/dictionary/culture on 2019, June 14.

2. *Baker's Evangelical Dictionary of Biblical Theology*, s.v. "Crown," Bible Study Tools, accessed June 17, 2019, https://www.biblestudytools.com/dictionary/crown/ on 2019, June 17.

3. Kevin Prosch, "So Come," recorded April 1991, in Even So Come A Live Night Of Worship, Kevin Prosch, Vineyard Ministries International, 1991, CD (see full lyrics below).

You have taken the precious
From the worthless and given us
Beauty for ashes, love for hate
You have chosen the weak things
Of the world to shame that which
*   is strong*
And foolish things to shame
*   the wise*
You are help to the helpless
Strength to the stranger
And a father to the child who's
*   left alone*
You've invited the thirsty
To come to the waters
And those who have no money
*   come and buy*
So come

So come
So come
So come
Behold the days are coming
For the Lord has promised
That the plowman will overtake
*   the reaper*
And our hearts will be the
*   threshing floor*
And the move of God we've cried
*   out for will come,*
It will surely come
For you will shake the heavens
And fill your house with glory
And turn the shame of outcasts
*   into praise*

Chapter 6

A Practical Guide to Soaking

I want to help you to develop a habit of spending quality time just loving Jesus. There is nothing more valuable than time with Him. Your relationship with the Lord will always be worth your time. This chapter looks at the practical elements of soaking, along with questions or problems you may come up against. Use this as a guide to refer back to as you learn to soak.

MAKE A QUIET SPACE

Most people need to learn how to be still in the presence of God. They're used to filling the silence with their worship and prayer. When God spoke to Elijah in First Kings 19, it wasn't in the thunder or in the whirlwind; it was that still, small voice. It's so important to find a quiet, still space to make room to hear God speaking and to recognize His presence.

> Most people need to learn how to be still in the presence of God. They're used to filling the silence with their worship and prayer.

Whether it's in your bedroom, or on your favorite chair in the living room, somewhere that's quiet and free from distractions is ideal. I've known friends who would rather lie on the floor than in their bed because they don't want to risk falling asleep. As you practice soaking, you'll get to know what works best for you.

Once you're comfortable, close your eyes and welcome the Holy Spirit. Fix your eyes on Jesus and tell Him that you love Him and want to spend time with Him.

When you get practiced at soaking you'll be able to more easily connect with the presence of God wherever you are.

I've soaked in the car, my garden, on trains and airplanes. I've learned that I can close myself off to the world around me and focus on Jesus.

> As you sing to Him, it will help you focus in on Him and bring your heart into peace. Starting with adoration and worship will help you take your focus from the distractions and busyness of life and onto Jesus.

LISTEN TO MUSIC

Music helps set a peaceful atmosphere as you soak. I love to start with worship music that draws my heart to loving Jesus. I wouldn't recommend using upbeat, joyful praise songs, but rather intimate songs that will facilitate your heart to connecting with His. Songs that you can really love Him with. As you sing to Him, it will help you focus in on Him and bring your heart into peace. Starting with adoration and worship will help you take your focus from the distractions and busyness of life and onto Jesus.

As you worship and feel the presence of the Lord permeating you, welcome Him even more. Recognize His presence with you. Tell Him that you love Him and you want to spend time with Him. Then allow Him to take the lead. Ask Him what He wants to do today and what He wants to show you.

At first, soaking to music with words is better because it helps you stay on track. Your mind can be incredibly busy and lyrics that direct you to rest and focus on Jesus will keep reminding you that you're there to connect with the Lord.

Your spirit is supposed to lead your life, not your soul.

After you've been soaking for a while, you might like to try using background music with no lyrics. I find that it allows more freedom in following where the Holy Spirit wants to lead you as you soak.

Managing Distractions

When you begin to soak, your mind will go nuts. As soon as you make a quiet space, you'll all of a sudden remember all the things you need to do and all the things you've forgotten. It can be so frustrating! Sometimes it's the devil distracting you and sometimes it's just your mind wanting to be in control.

According to First Thessalonians 5:23, we're all made up of a spirit, soul, and body. Your spirit is the part of you that is made new when you give your life to Jesus and it's the part of you that communicates with God. Your soul is made up of your mind, your will, and your emotions. Most people live their lives controlled by their soul. They follow where their mind, their will, or their emotions lead them. That becomes a problem when you come to soak. Your soul, and specifically your mind, is so used to being in control, that it can be challenging at first when you try to connect spirit to Spirit with the Lord.

Your spirit is supposed to lead your life, not your soul. Each of us is meant to be aligned in order of spirit, soul, and body. Your own spirit lines up under the Holy Spirit, then the soul and the body under that. You can thank your soul and body because they're really incredible, but take authority and tell them to come under subjection to your spirit, which is under subjection to the Spirit of God.

Then, when distractions come, take a piece of paper, write it down, and go back to soaking. I always thank the Lord when I get one of these little reminders. It may have been the enemy trying to distract me, or my mind trying to take control, but I'd rather give the Lord the credit! When I first started soaking, it took me three weeks to get my mind in obedience.

If the thoughts of everything you have to do are causing you stress, picture yourself giving them to Jesus as you write them down. Take a deep breath and ask Him to take care of those things and to show you what to do with them after you've finished soaking. Psalm 55:22 says, *"Cast your cares on the Lord and He will sustain you"* (NIV). He is so able to take care of all of your needs and help you with every little challenge you may face. He will give you the strength you need and the best thing you can do is draw on His strength by continuing to spend time with Him, rather than getting up and running around, trying to complete all the tasks that are on your mind.

> As you continue to soak it'll become such a sweet time that you'll find yourself drawn to soak for longer and longer.

Sometimes Jesus does remind you of the important things that you need to remember while you soak. If that happens, thank Him, write it down, and ask Him what else He's saying.

When you get distracted, refocus yourself by worshipping. Worship reminds your soul what you are there for. Tell Jesus, "Lord, I love you. I'm here for you. I fix my eyes on you again. You are worthy of my worship."

How Long to Soak

When you begin to soak, start with something that you can do consistently every day, perhaps 10 to 15 minutes at a time. If you're super busy and can't soak every day, try five days a week, but be as consistent as possible. Learning to soak is about building a habit. It's also about getting to know the presence of God and building a relationship with Him.

It's important not to compare yourself or try to soak for an hour each day when you start off. Your mind will probably go all over the place, you'll just get frustrated with the process, and you'll stop doing it. Regularity is key, so choose a routine that you can keep up with.

As you continue to soak it'll become such a sweet time that you'll find yourself drawn to soak for longer and longer.

I used to have marathon soaking session where I'd take three days, get together with a girlfriend, and we'd soak from 9 A.M. until 6 P.M. It was amazing how the Holy Spirit would come. Not everybody can do that because we've all got different personalities. The idea is not to count the hours you've completed in a week. It's more about the attitude of your heart, wanting to spend time with the Lord, to love Him and to hear what He has to say to you.

> **When we position ourselves to be childlike and receive our heavenly Father's good gifts, we get to receive the kingdom of Heaven!**

No Agendas

When you soak, the only priority is being together with the Lord. Try to put your own agendas aside and let yourself be His Beloved. Ask the Holy Spirit where He wants to take you today and welcome His presence. You'll be surprised where He takes you.

Jesus told us to be like little children. That's the attitude that we need to have when we soak. Soaking is a vulnerable and humble thing to do. Our minds tell us that it's foolish to be vulnerable, but Jesus said, *"Truly I tell you, unless you change and become like little children, you will never enter the kingdom of heaven. Therefore, whoever takes the lowly position of this child is the greatest in the kingdom of heaven"* (Matthew 18:3-4 NIV). When we position ourselves to be child-like and receive our heavenly Father's good gifts, we get to receive the kingdom of Heaven!

If God seems to be repeating Himself, don't get frustrated. Simply ask Him why. It could be that God wants to remind you of His heart for you until you really believe it.

HOW TO RECORD WHAT GOD DOES

As you soak, God will speak. It's important to tune your heart to be able to hear what He has to say and to learn to see what He's showing you. In Chapter 3, I explained Mark Virkler's four keys to hearing God's voice. Hearing God's voice is a learning process. When you get a vision, even if it's a little bit, don't analyze it. Let God lead you where He wants to.

It's good to have a journal and write down some of the things that He tells you so that you can pray them back, ponder them, and meditate on them. I often try to draw out what happened or jot down notes to jog my memory. Sometimes I'll be reminded of someone, so I'll make a note of their name and ask the Holy Spirit whether I need to call them later or take time to pray for them.

If God seems to be repeating Himself, don't get frustrated. Simply ask Him why. It could be that God wants to remind you of His heart for you until you really believe it. God wants to tell you that He loves you over and over again. God is love and He loves you. He wants your heart, your mind, your will, and your emotions to know that.

WHAT IF NOTHING HAPPENS?

It might seem like you speak and nothing happens. You might not feel, hear, or see anything. That's okay! Even if you don't see anything happen, soaking is not a waste of time.

Even if you don't see anything happen, soaking is not a waste of time.

God values your choice to be with Him so much! If that's you, keep on practicing and don't give up. God likes persistence. He likes it when we pursue Him.

In Matthew 7, Jesus said, *"Ask, and it will be given to you; seek, and you will find; knock, and it will be opened to you. For everyone who asks receives, and he who seeks finds, and to him who knocks it will be opened"* (Matthew 7:7-8). As you seek the presence of the Holy Spirit, He is delighted to show Himself to you.

Remember that your heavenly Father wants to give you good gifts, so much more than any good and loving father would want to. He wants an intimate relationship with you far more than you could imagine. Keep asking Him for more. It's that simple prayer that we learned to pray when the revival began: "More, Holy Spirit!"

It's not about doing it perfectly. God is interested in your heart.

We had one pastor from the United States come for three weeks back when we were running nightly meetings. In that whole three weeks, he didn't feel a thing. He was totally discouraged, but he continued to soak in faith that God was doing something. When he went home, he told his church what he saw in Toronto. He said, "I don't think I received anything, but if you want me to pray for you, come up." The whole church came up to the front, and as he prayed for them, the presence of God came so mightily that they all fell to the ground. The pastor was so excited that he jumped on an airplane and came back to tell us what happened!

WHAT IF I FALL ASLEEP?

This is a question I've heard many times. I'm sure most people who soak regularly have fallen asleep while soaking at one point. I don't think there's a problem with that. Perhaps you might fall asleep because you're really tired and you really needed deep rest in the presence of God. God is able to speak to you in dreams, too!

It's not about doing it perfectly. God is interested in your heart. Do you want to be with Him, to spend time with Him?

It's not about accomplishing tasks or meeting a time quota. It's about a relationship with Him. In 2019, John and I were teaching at the London School of Theology. During a ministry time, one of the graduating students laid down to soak and immediately fell asleep. When I invited people up for testimony, he shared what had happened, and I initially thought it was rather odd to testify that you'd slept all the way through soaking! Then he went on to tell us what a miracle it was

If you're in a wilderness season, there can be some blockages that the Lord is revealing in you that He wants to deal with.

because he'd had difficulty sleeping at night for years and years and would normally only get two or three hours of sleep each night. The next morning he testified again that he had slept for eight hours the night before. He was absolutely radiant.

If you realize that you're falling asleep more frequently than you'd like when you soak, you might want to try soaking in a different position, like sitting upright or lying on the floor rather than on a comfortable sofa or bed. You could also try soaking at a different time of day. If you soak in the evening and find you're too sleepy, try soaking in the morning, or earlier in the evening before you get too tired.

MANAGING THROUGH DRY SEASONS

You might find yourself in a dry season, where you struggle to connect with the presence of God like you did before. For me, that was at the same time I was ill for almost three years. Everything that I did before to connect with the Lord, didn't seem to work. It was like I could feel His presence near but not really close. I knew He hadn't left me, but it was the first time I had to learn to trust in faith that He was with me when my feelings and experiences didn't line up with that.

I continued to soak and to read the Word and I really examined my heart. I asked the Lord, "Is there something that I need to deal with? What do I need to work through?" If you're in a wilderness season, there can be some blockages that the Lord is revealing in you that He wants to deal with. We all need seasons of healing in our hearts and our emotions.

When I met Dr. Arne Elsen from Germany, I learned to use the worship timer that reminded me to worship every 10 minutes. The worship timer is a great tool to help you refocus quickly back on the Lord. When you're struggling through a difficult time, it's easy to become very inward focused. You spend so much time and energy dealing with the problems that you lose sight of God's goodness. If you're sick, if you're discouraged, or if you're in a wilderness season, make the decision to praise the Lord. Bless Him, no matter what you feel like. As you turn your focus to Him, you'll feel His attention on you too.

ARE SOME PEOPLE BETTER AT RESTING THAN OTHERS?

We're all wired differently. Some people will find it much easier to soak for 30 minutes than others. Some people are so action oriented that staying still for a long period of time is difficult. Soaking doesn't have to be in a horizontal, lying-down position. For many people, it helps to stay still, but if

> For many people, it helps to stay still, but if you struggle to focus when you're still, then you can still soak while you're on the move.

you struggle to focus when you're still, then you can still soak while you're on the move. You can quiet yourself down and tune your mind to what the Holy Spirit is saying and doing while you go for a walk, ride your bike, or exercise at the gym. The important thing is getting that heart-to-heart connection with Him.

Heidi Baker soaks in God's presence while she snorkels in the ocean. It doesn't matter what your body is doing, as long as your mind can come under subjection to your spirit and you can connect with God.

FAITH AND FEELINGS

John has much more of a faith gifting than I do. He knows that God's going to fill him as he spends time with Him, whether he feels it or not. He comes into agreement with God's Word. But it took John a long time to learn to sense the Holy Spirit and trust what His presence felt like and that what he was feeling was really Him. I rely much more on my prophetic intuition as the Lord leads . I can sense how the Holy Spirit is moving and I'm constantly asking Him, "Where are you? What are you doing?"

Whether you struggle to sense God or need to learn to rely on faith for what God is doing, on both ends of the spectrum there's an important learning and growing process that we all need to go through.

If you're like John and have a faith gifting, or you're gifted as a teacher, a producer, or strategist, you may need to learn to tune in and to sense the Holy Spirit. On the other hand, I had to learn when I felt sick or when I didn't feel the Holy Spirit, that He is good and He is still here. I had to learn much more to walk by faith.

The Bible says that everything we receive from God is by faith and not by feelings (see Gal. 3:14). At the same time, God also relates to us through our senses and feelings. Whether you struggle to sense God or need to learn to rely on faith for what God is doing, on both ends of the spectrum there's an important learning and growing process that we all need to go through.

SOAKING PRAYER FOR OTHERS

When God's presence comes strongly in a meeting, people will often fall down when they receive prayer. But I've noticed that people can't seem to stay and rest in that presence. They get prayer and within a few minutes, they are on their way. It's one of my pet peeves.

There is so much more of Him to experience than just falling down. He wants to connect with each person on a deep

heart level. He wants to know if they really value His presence enough to stay and wait on Him. That's why I always encourage people to stay soaking when they've received prayer. You can also continue to pray for people while they lie down and soak. Simply lay a hand on them and pray quietly. Welcome the Holy Spirit and pray as you feel led. Even if they don't fall down, encourage them to find somewhere to lie down and position themselves before the Lord. There's no magic in falling. The

> There is so much more of Him to experience than just falling down. He wants to connect with each person on a deep heart level.

real value is in making space for the Lord, telling Him that you want more of Him and you're here for Him.

When you're ministering to someone, encourage them that even if they don't feel anything, God is at work.

Encourage them to ask God what He's doing in them and not to compare themselves with what God is doing in someone else. It's easy to notice the people who are shaking or manifesting and think that because that's not happening to you, you're not receiving anything. Remind them that we receive from God by faith and remind them to keep their focus on adoring Jesus and worshipping Him.

John and I will often coach people to look for the peace of God in their heart. If you are busy praying or trying too hard to receive, you need to take a deep breath, let all striving go and come into rest. Remember what we say, "Quiet yourself down, fix your eyes on Jesus and tune in to the spontaneous flow of His presence."

ACTIVATION

What are your challenges to connecting with God's presence and resting with Him?

Do you tell yourself, "I'm not good at resting" or, "I'm just not built to sense and feel the Holy Spirit," or, "I'll always be distracted?" If that's you, tell Him:

> *Lord, here I am. I repent of believing that because of my character or personality, I can't spend time resting with you, or that I can't receive from you. Lord, I want you, whether or not I feel anything. I position myself in faith to receive from you.*

Chapter 7

SOAKING AND HEALING

I've never met anyone who doesn't want to get better when they're unwell. God wants us to be healthy too! He can heal every sickness and disease. We all probably know someone who needs healing. It may be for aches and pains, a broken bone, or something more serious like a long-term illness or even cancer. The church is waking up to the power of healing prayer. All over the world, people are choosing in faith to pray for healing and miracles are happening. We all want to be effective when we pray for healing.

INSTANT HEALING?

Our culture demands things to be instant. We're used to getting everything we need straightaway. If there's a lineup for coffee at a drive thru, we get frustrated. We shop online, expecting the order to arrive the next day. Magazines are full of instant weight-loss solutions, promising us miraculous results without any hard work.

We can become that way with Jesus. We want Him to instantly fix our problems, our finances, our emotional trauma, and our physical ailments. In reality, all these things require commitment. Knowing Jesus intimately doesn't happen at the snap of a finger. It's the same with healing emotional trauma. It takes time for your heart to be healed. You get a measure of healing, then you walk that out, and then the

Holy Spirit will deal with more. John and I have made a commitment to regularly take time to get inner healing and make ourselves accountable. It's helped us stay emotionally healthy and minister out of a place of wholeness throughout the years.

I was recently ministering in Charlotte, North Carolina, when a woman came up to me. She told me she needed deliverance, that she was hearing voices, and she gave me a long list of what was wrong with her. She wanted me to give her some sort

Inner healing is a process we all need to commit to as the Holy Spirit guides.

of instant fix. I just hugged her, prayed for her, and said, "Honey, let's ask the people here for a good counsellor." What she needed was to walk the journey of inner healing, rather than find a quick solution. Inner healing is a process we all need to commit to as the Holy Spirit guides.

Let's look again at John 15:7: *"If you abide in Me, and My words abide in you, you will ask what you desire, and it shall be done for you."* We crave instant solutions, but Jesus calls us to abide in Him. That takes time. It's the same with physical healing. Sometimes when we pray for others, there's instant healing, but I've found that it can be incredibly effective to soak people in prayer for healing.

HEALING SOAKING PRAYER

When the revival began, I quickly fell in love with soaking people in prayer. I used to spend hours at a time praying for people as they rested in God's presence and we'd see amazing things happening.

When someone would come up for healing prayer, as I prayed I would check in with them and see how they were feeling. Often, they'd have a measure of healing, but still have some pain or remaining issues. I'd just ask the Holy Spirit, "Lord, is there something going on here? Something blocking their healing?" Sometimes He'd get me to ask the person if they had anger toward somebody, if they had unforgiveness, or if there was a trauma around the situation. That would reveal an area where they needed to forgive or repent of a judgment, which would unlock greater healing or breakthrough for the person.

It was around this time that John and I heard about Francis MacNutt's healing ministry through soaking prayer. We got in touch with Francis and his wife Judith and did some conferences together. What they were doing was the same kind of prayer as I'd been learning, but they'd begun to teach and write about it and we learned a lot from them. They spent hours and hours, even days, soaking people in prayer for healing. They saw incredible results just by taking time with a person and continuously praying over them. Francis talked about how healing can happen instantly and that we're going to see a day when all healing miracles are instant, just like Jesus. However, until we get to that level of anointing, Francis had found that soaking prayer was an incredibly effective way to see people healed.

The MacNutts also valued healing of the heart. They reinforced the importance of listening to the Holy Spirit to find out if any judgments, trauma, or unforgiveness was blocking the healing.

FORGIVENESS AND HEALING

When we choose to judge or not to forgive another person, it can block our healing. In Matthew 6:14-15, Jesus said, *"For if you forgive other people when they sin against you, your heavenly Father will also forgive you. But if you do not forgive others their sins, your Father will not forgive your sins"* (NIV). Through Jesus, we have received forgiveness for our unjust behaviour and sins and been given grace and mercy that we don't deserve.

> **When we choose to judge or not to forgive another person, it can block our healing.**

When someone hurts us, we want justice for what they did. But when we choose not to forgive them, we reap what we sow. We stay in the place of justice, which is the enemy's camp. There, he can demand that we pay for what we owe. It gives satan a legal right over our healing. Instead, we need to forgive. Jesus has given us incredible grace, so we must give that grace to others too. As I've ministered healing to people, I've simply asked them, "Do you need to forgive the other driver in the accident?" or, "Do you need to forgive yourself for your part in this?" This can reveal that they have unforgiveness toward themselves or another person. When we pray that simple forgiveness prayer, often something physical shifts too. It's incredible!

John and I were once in Australia teaching. We were beginning ministry when John had a word of knowledge and asked, "Is there anybody here that has had pain from an accident for 30 years or more?" A pastor's wife put her hand up, came up to the front and told us, "When I was 16, I was riding a horse. He tripped and I fell off the horse and the horse fell on me. It absolutely wrecked my hips and my whole skeletal frame." We prayed for her and we asked her if she'd ever forgiven herself. She said, "That day I went riding when my parents told me I couldn't. I disobeyed them and went anyway. I need to forgive myself because it was my fault." So she forgave herself and we prayed for her. She was about two-thirds better instantly.

It was amazing, but there was still some pain that wasn't healed. I prayed and asked the Lord what else we needed to do. I had an intersecting thought that she needed to forgive the horse. I was a little skeptical but I went ahead and asked her, "What did you say when the horse fell on you?" Of course, she had gotten really angry with the horse. I asked her if she'd ever forgiven the horse and she replied, "No, I haven't because I blamed him and myself for all my pain." She forgave the horse, and instantly, the rest of the pain went. She was totally healed!

Years later, I saw her in England at a conference. She came up and said, "I'm the lady who needed to forgive the horse. I wanted to tell you, I have never had one single ounce of pain since that day." It's so incredible that the simple act of forgiving herself and her horse completely changed her life. She had pain from the accident for over 30 years, and in a moment she was completely free. God is so good.

WAIT AND PERSIST

There are some great biblical examples of persisting for healing. When you pray for someone and wait on God, sometimes He'll ask you to do something that is out of your paradigm. In Second Kings 4, we read the story of Elisha, the Shunammite woman, and her son. The Shunammite woman fed Elisha when he would come by and even made a room in her house for him. Elisha wanted to give her something back. She had no children, and Elisha prophesied that she'd have a son the following year.

She had a son, and a few years later he died. So the, Shunammite woman left her son at her house and took a donkey to find Elisha. She met Elisha's servant Gehazi first. He asked her what was wrong, but the woman told him nothing was wrong. She kept going, got to the feet of Elisha and wouldn't let him go. She told Elisha that her son was dead and Elisha told his servant to take a staff and put it on the boy. But the, Shunammite woman persisted with Elisha until he came back to her house with her.

When Elisha got to the house, he prayed and paced back and forth. The Lord told Elisha to lie on the dead body of the boy, mouth to mouth and hand to hand. The boy's body became warm but he didn't come back to life. Elisha prayed again and God told him to lie on the boy a second time. The boy sneezed and came back to life. Both Elisha and the Shunammite woman were persistent and the boy was healed.

Jesus persisted when He healed the blind man in Mark 8:22-25.. The blind man asked to be healed by Jesus. Jesus didn't do it right there but led the man out of town first. Jesus spat on his eyes and put His hand on them. The blind man had a measure of healing but couldn't see fully yet. Then Jesus put His hands on the man again and his eyesight was completely restored. That's a great example

> **When you pray for healing, take risks and follow the Holy Spirit's nudges. It might mean that you do something unusual and unexpected or that you need to wait and keep persisting.**

of Jesus following the Father for what to do and what to say. When you pray for healing, take risks and follow the Holy Spirit's nudges. It might mean that you do something unusual and unexpected, or that you need to wait and keep persisting.

FORGIVING HER FATHER

One of the first times I saw radical healing through soaking was with Chloe Glassborow. In 2003, John and I were ministering in Bath, England at a conference about the Father's love. Chloe and her husband Stuart, were skeptical of what was going on at the conference, but Stuart was desperate for Chloe to be healed and he felt that God was asking him to bring her. The doctors had told Chloe that she'd be in a wheelchair by the time she was 30. She had arthritis since she was a child and she was having multiple epileptic seizures a day. She was lactose intolerant, had cystic ovaries, and had daily migraines.

Chloe came to the meeting in Bath, digging in her heels. She had a very difficult relationship with her father and didn't want to be at a conference that was talking about God as Father. They came and sat in the back row. That night, we were teaching on grace and forgiveness and we called people up for ministry. Chloe says in her testimony that she found herself at the front, almost involuntarily.

As we led people through forgiving their parents, I heard her wailing so loudly that I came off the platform to minister to her. She had begun to forgive her father for all the pain he had caused in her life. As I prayed, she fell over in the Spirit and I felt like I should stay with her. I spent some time praying through her father issues with her. Then the Lord said, "Ask her if she needs healing." So I said, "Are you sick? Do you need healing?" She started to list it all to me: "I can't walk upstairs. My husband has to carry me up and I come down the stairs on my bottom. I'm almost in a wheelchair." I prayed for her and soaked her for a little bit.

After a while, she began to feel burning hot, so I got her to stand up and see if anything was changing. She stood up and I asked her to see if she could test to see if she was healed. The church we were in, Bath City Church, has really steep stairs up to a high platform. All of a sudden, she walked right to the top of those stairs. It was spectacular! She was completely healed and it was so simple. She chose radical forgiveness toward her father and then I soaked her in the presence of God and she was completely transformed.

Afterward, she went to her doctor and told him what had happened. She was on such a high dosage of epilepsy medication that he wouldn't take her off it immediately but agreed to reduce it over a year. Within that year, she totally came off all the medication she was on and has never had a seizure since. She and her husband Stu are now in the senior leadership team of Catch The Fire. They're incredible apostolic leaders, radically impacting the UK and beyond. She is so different from the woman I met all those years ago, and it's through the power of Jesus!

LITTLE BY LITTLE

A few years ago, a pastor from our Partners in Harvest network named Yvonne Brett had a terrible accident that damaged her brain, causing her to have a stroke. Yvonne felt that the Lord was telling her to visit Toronto, so she told her doctor that she wanted to go. She was living in Virginia, but the doctor told her she couldn't fly and that driving wouldn't be safe. They'd already seen other blood clots in her brain, which meant that she was at risk of having another stroke, which could have been fatal. Yvonne still really wanted to go, so her husband got a van, they put a mattress in the back, and she laid down for the whole journey north to Toronto.

They came to a meeting and John saw her but had forgotten about the accident. He called her up to the front and asked the speaker, Larry Randolph, to prophesy over her. Larry gave her a word and prayed for her and she fell down under the power of the Spirit. While Yvonne was on the stage, I saw her hand and leg that were disabled from the stroke and asked if I could soak her. She agreed and I stayed on the platform with her and soaked her in prayer.

After a while, the Lord told me to put my finger in her hand that was tightly shut. I stuck my finger in her fist and continued to pray for Yvonne while worshipping Jesus quietly, as Larry Randolph was speaking. Finally, the Lord told me to tell her to move her fingers. I said, "Yvonne, move your fingers." She replied, "I can't move them." I said, "The Lord told you to move your fingers, so give it a try." She was really unsure but eventually, she tried and I felt her fingers move a tiny fraction.

I told her what I felt, "Yvonne, you moved your fingers, a tiny little bit. You can move them!" But she said, "Oh no, I can't move them." We had a conversation back and forth on the stage for about 10 minutes, and eventually, she began to try again to move her hand. The skin on her hand had started out a pasty, grayish colour, but then we could see the blood coming back into it. That gave her more faith and she started to move her fingers more. The next thing I knew, she was lifting her arm and waving her hand!

Then I said, "Now, move your foot. Lift your leg." She said, "Well, I can't." We went back and forth again as I encouraged her that the Lord was doing something in her body. Gradually, she moved her foot a little bit, then a little bit more. I said, "Yvonne, it's moving! Keep going, keep moving it. God is healing you." Not long after that, she was swinging her leg. She got up off the ground and right in the middle of the sermon, she started dancing. Her husband was standing there saying, "That's my wife. She can't do that!"

The same power that raised Jesus from the dead, the Spirit of God, filled her body and brought complete new life.

What an incredible miracle! The same power that raised Jesus from the dead, the Spirit of God, filled her body and brought complete new life. All I did was spend 45 minutes praying with her, just marinating her in the presence of God, and God healed her. It's so simple and we can all do that. When we're filled with His presence, we can take the time and partner with God to soak people back to life.

We need to learn obedience to the voice of God. When He whispers and asks you to do something, be like a child and trust your Father. At the beginning, the Holy Spirit asked me to put my finger in Yvonne's hand, which might seem like a strange thing to do, but her healing actually began in her hand. Let yourself be filled with the presence of God and take the time to partner with Him to soak people back to life.

STAGE-FOUR CANCER

The first time I taught on healing through soaking, I was in England at a Revival Alliance conference. I gave the group a basic introduction to soaking, then told some healing testimonies. Then I led them through a soaking session.

A lady had come to the conference with stage-four cancer, but had no money for a ticket. My granddaughter Jessica had welcomed her in and she ended up in my session. I didn't know that the lady was there. After we soaked, I asked for testimonies and she was the first one up. She said, "I was so sick. I was in so much pain. The girl at the door let me in. I came to your session and then you told me to lie on the floor. I was just absolutely furious with you, because I was in so much pain. I saw other people doing it and I really wanted to be healed. So I decided to lie on the floor even though I was in excruciating pain."

I had told them that we'd soak for about 15 minutes. The lady told me, "It was probably about the 12-minute mark that I realized the pain is gone. I have no pain." She couldn't believe it so she felt her stomach where she'd had a huge tumour that made her look like she was pregnant. The tumour was gone! Nobody had prayed for her. She just positioned herself before the Lord, laid down, and asked for her healing, which was a brave thing to do, considering how much pain she was in. As she soaked, the Lord healed her of her pain and took away her tumour. It was completely miraculous. Everyone in the room was so excited to see that miracle take place through soaking.

When Healing Doesn't Happen

Sometimes when we pray healing happens instantly, but sometimes it doesn't. That can be so discouraging. If we're not healed instantly, we can lose hope and our faith goes way down. We start to ask, "What's wrong with me? Why can't I get healed?" We lose sight of God and stop looking for His perspective in our situation. Sometimes, healing takes a long time. That was my experience. I had to keep holding on to God throughout years of one sickness after another.

When healing doesn't happen, we have to keep trusting God. In Genesis, we see that Joseph had a long and difficult road to the place that he knew God was leading him. Joseph was estranged from his family, he was made a slave, he was accused of something he didn't do, and he was in prison for 13 years. In all of that, he kept his heart right before the Lord. He didn't complain and he didn't get bitter.

If you've been praying and believing for a healing or a breakthrough, don't lose hope. Don't lose sight of God's goodness even in the most difficult times in your life. Keep holding on to Him and trusting in His Word. Jesus is the model that we follow for healing because everyone He ministered to was completely healed. That means that healing is always possible. I want to encourage you to keep a childlike heart and believe that God can still heal you. He can bring about your breakthrough in a moment, just like He did with Joseph when he was taken out of prison and given authority over the nation of Egypt.

Have you been disappointed when you have prayed and believed for someone to be healed and not seen any breakthrough? God knows your heart and wants to restore your hope today.

ACTIVATION

Have you been disappointed when you have prayed and believed for someone to be healed and not seen any breakthrough? God knows your heart and wants to restore your hope today. If that's you, pray this from your heart:

God, it has been difficult seeing the people I love suffer from sickness and not be healed in the timing that I hoped for. I've been disappointed and lost hope. I'm sorry for any lies that I have believed. God, would You renew my hope and faith for healing again? I want to see from Your perspective. I believe that it's always Your will to heal, so would You give me childlike faith to believe for healing again.

Do you need healing? As you soak, ask the Lord to heal your body:

Lord, You say that if we ask, You will answer. So, Lord, I ask today that You would come, that You would fill me and that You would allow me to love You and let You love me. I'm going to position myself today for healing. I ask You, Lord, to heal me, as I rest in Your presence.

Chapter 8

RESOURCES

I'm excited for you to use this book as a launchpad into a greater relationship with God. Here are some resources that will help you continue on your journey of soaking and deeper intimacy. Of course there are many, many more anointed and wonderful resources that will help lead you, these are just a small sample of a few favorites.

MUSIC

When I soak, I choose songs that draw me into loving Jesus. I find that many albums have one or two songs that are good for soaking, so I suggest that you build your own playlists of songs for soaking. Here are some of my personal favorites:

Bethel Music has released some great albums that I've made playlists from, including *Victory* (2019), *We Will Not Be Shaken* (2015) and *Be Lifted High* (2011). They've also released two albums, which are beautiful compilations of Bethel worship songs without any singing or lyrics.

Catch the Fire Music's latest album *Presence* (2019) has some incredible songs for soaking, including Jonathan Clarke's "Affection Devotion" and Chris and Summer Shealy singing "What a Father." Also, check out the album *Everything Comes Alive* including Benjamin Jackson's song "You Shall Reign" and Alice Clarke's "Everything Comes Alive."

Terry MacAlmon has released many albums with piano-based worship and soaking music. He has contemplative worship and instrumental worship on his albums *The Refreshing, Vol. 1* (2015) and *The Refreshing, Vol. 2: Symphony of Love* (2016)

Alberto and Kimberly Rivera are a husband and wife team who have come to Toronto many times to minister in worship. Their music is spontaneous and presence-based, which makes it perfect for soaking. They have released four albums specifically for soaking sessions and many instrumental albums too.

I love **Bryan and Katie Torwalt's** worship music. I often begin soaking with their song "Holy Spirit" (2011). Their EP *Praise Before My Breakthrough* (2018) has a wonderful selection of songs for resting and receiving from God.

Laura Woodley Osman's album has *Home* been a favorite of mine for soaking for years. Many of her albums combine peaceful music and prayers to help you focus your heart on Jesus. In 2015, Laura released *Story of All Stories* an album written for children, but has incredible music that people of any age can soak with.

BOOKS

I've covered many subjects in this book that you can explore more deeply, such as hearing God's voice, dreams and visions, getting to know the Holy Spirit, understanding the Father's love, and building intimacy with Jesus. If you're looking to go deeper, here are some great books:

John and Carol Arnott, *Grace and Forgiveness*

John and Carol Arnott, *Preparing for the Glory*

Chris DuPre, *The Wild Love of God*

Jack Frost, *Experiencing the Father's Embrace*

Jeanne Guyon, *Experiencing the Depths of Jesus Christ*

Peter Herbeck, *When the Spirit Comes in Power*

Benny Hinn, *Good Morning, Holy Spirit*

John Paul Jackson, *Understanding Dreams and Visions*

Beni Johnson, *The Power of Communion*

A.J. Jones, *Finding Father*

James Jordan, *Sonship: A Journey into Father's Heart*

Chester and Betsy Kylstra, *Biblical Healing and Deliverance*

Brennan Manning, *The Ragamuffin Gospel*

Andrew Murray, *The Master's Indwelling*

Henri J.M. Nouwen, *The Way of the Heart*

Ed Piorek, *The Central Event*

Mark Virkler and Charity Virkler Kayembe,
Hearing God Through Your Dreams

Mark Virkler, *4 Keys to Hearing God's Voice*

INNER HEALING

I can't emphasize enough how important it is that we all pursue the healing and restoration of our hearts. When you don't deal with your past hurts, they don't just disappear. Your issues prevent you from fulfilling your God-given destiny and cause you to continue living out unhealthy cycles. When we deal with the issues of our hearts, we become more like Jesus and we're able to love Him and others more effectively.

Forgiveness is a core part of inner healing, so I recommend you get a copy of our book *Grace and Forgiveness* and begin to forgive those who have hurt you.

Our Catch The Fire churches have **Schools of Ministry** where you can spend five months or a year letting God minister to you and transform your heart. I highly recommend the three-week Leaders School at Catch The Fire in Toronto. It's an amazing place for leaders to receive refreshing and healing. Find out more at www.somtoronto.com.

Restoring the Foundations is an excellent inner-healing ministry. Restoring the Foundations has ministers all over the world who are trained to lead you through a personal ministry week that will go deep in your heart to restore your life and relationships. John and I have had many Restoring the Foundations ministry weeks throughout our life. We've also had almost everyone we work with go through this ministry! We love how it's transformed our lives and the lives of people we know and love. Find out more at www .restoringthefoundations.org.

There are many other inner-healing ministries with great reputations and success that you can receive from, including **Bethel Sozo**, **HeartSync**, and **Trauma**.

GUIDED SOAKING AND INSPIRATION

In the early days, we established soaking centres all over the world where people could gather together and receive the presence of God. Often, a leader would take the group through soaking by selecting prayers, music, and scriptures. These soaking centres are no longer officially running, but that doesn't have to stop you from gathering together with friends to soak. If you're looking for inspiration as you soak alone, or together with others, I've put together some scriptures and prayers.

Soaking at the Beginning of the Day

> *Prayer: Good morning, Holy Spirit! I welcome You. Jesus, I love You so much. I worship You. Lord, I want to take this time to position my heart before You, at the start of this day. I want You to be the center of my day. There may be a lot going on today, but Lord, would You help me put my busy thoughts on hold so that I can position myself for love right now. I love You so much. My relationship with You is so important. It's more important than all my plans for today. Show me Your love. Draw me close to You. What do You want to say to me?*

> SCRIPTURE: PSALM 42:7-8

Soaking on a Busy Day

Prayer: Lord, today is a busy day. You know everything that is going on in my life. Father, I give it all back into Your hands. Would You dust off all the busyness and all the stress. I quiet myself down and position myself before You now. I invite You to come, Holy Spirit, and fill me. I want to spend this time in loving You. There is a lot going on in my life right now, but You are far more important. I tell my mind to be still. I choose to receive from You and know that You are God. I give You all the burdens that feel so heavy and I'm asking for Your deep rest in my soul.

SCRIPTURE: MATTHEW 11:28-30

Soaking at the End of the Day

Prayer: Father, thank You for today. Thank You that You have been present all throughout today. You've seen the busy moments and the quiet moments. You've seen all of my thoughts and my actions. Thank You that You love me through it all. I take a deep breath, and as I breathe out, I give everything back to You. I want to connect with You. Holy Spirit, I welcome Your peace to come over me now. I tell my mind to be still.

Lord, I come under the shadow of Your wings. You are my help and my strength. I come to rest in Your presence today.

SCRIPTURE: PSALM 63:6-8

Soaking for Healing

Prayer: God, thank You that You are an incredible Father. Thank You that You provide all of my needs. Jesus, thank You that on the cross You paid for all my sin, sickness, disease and pain. Isaiah 53:5 says, "by His stripes we are healed. "You know that I need healing today. I'm asking for Your healing presence to come and fill me as I soak. I choose to quiet down every racing thought, every fear, and every lie that would stop me from connecting with You and receiving from You. I trust You to take care of me. Show me how to respond to what You're doing as I rest in Your presence. If there's anyone I need to forgive or anything I need to repent of, I'm willing to do it. Thank You Lord, that You want to heal me.

SCRIPTURE: LUKE 11:11-13

Soaking When You're in a Difficult Time

Prayer: Holy Spirit, I welcome You. I come to You today with heavy burdens. My heart is hurting. (Take some time to pour out your pain before God.) *Thank You, Lord, that You know my pain. God, I choose to praise You today before my breakthrough. I thank You that You are good, even when my circumstances are not. I want to experience Your comfort, Your kindness, and Your goodness today. Lord, I want a deep and intimate relationship with You. I want to know You as I walk through this valley.*

SCRIPTURE: PSALM 62:1-2, 5-8

Soaking with Your Spouse

Prayer: Father, we welcome You. Jesus, come and be with us. Holy Spirit, come and fill us. Lord, we've positioned ourselves as a couple to be with You today. You are the most important thing in our marriage. We can't do anything without You and without Your presence. We worship You. We want to be diligent about resting in You. We lay down all our priorities and needs for You. We give this time to You, Lord. Would You lead us and guide us?. Fill us with Your love, that we may love each other and those around us, as You love us.

SCRIPTURE: HEBREWS 4:9-11

Soaking in a Small Group

Prayer: God, we've come together today to encounter You. We choose to lay down every other agenda for You. We focus our hearts and minds on You, our wonderful Lord. Come, Holy Spirit. Come and fill us. We love You, Lord. Jesus, You are our beloved. We're here to wait on You and abide with You. Thank You that when we're thirsty, You give us a drink. We're hungry and thirsty for more of You. Thank You that You satisfy our souls with abundance. Thank You for Your presence with us as we gather. We're listening to what You have to say today.

SCRIPTURE: ISAIAH 55:1-3

Soaking Prayer for Others

Prayer: Holy Spirit, I welcome You. Father, thank You that You come and want to bless Your children. Thank You that You are kind, loving, and present. Would You come and fill this one now? Come and speak to them, heal them, and bless them. Lead them beside still waters today. Restore their soul. Let them drink deeply of Your loving presence. Fill them with comfort and joy in Your presence. Keep coming, Holy Spirit.

SCRIPTURE: PSALM 23

ABOUT CAROL ARNOTT

Carol Arnott, and her husband John, are the founding pastors of Catch the Fire—formerly known as the Toronto Airport Christian Fellowship—and overseers of the Catch the Fire Partners network of churches. As international speakers, John and Carol have become known for their ministry of revival in the context of the Father's saving and restoring love. As the Holy Spirit moves with signs and wonders, they have seen millions of lives touched and changed through God's power and Christ's love.